TRIATHLONS
FOR
KIDS

Books by Sally Edwards

Triathlons for Women (1992)
Triathlons for Kids (1992)
Triathlons for Fun (1992)
The Equilibrium Plan (1987)
Triathlon Training and Racing (1985)
The Woman Runner's Training Diary (1984)
The Triathlon Log (1983)
How to Organize a Triathlon (1983)
Triathlon: A Triple Fitness Sport (1982)

TRIATHLONS FOR KIDS

by Sally Edwards

A Triathlon Book Series

Published by Triathlete Magazine

Library of Congress Cataloging in
Publication Data

First printing: May 1992
Printed in the USA

Triathlete Magazine
Santa Monica, CA

Additional copies may be purchased by
sending a check for $9.00 for shipping
and handling (add applicable state sales
tax) to:

FLEET FEET PRESS
2408 "J" Street
Sacramento, CA 95816
(916) 442-3338

Acknowledgments

This book is dedicated to opportunity:

the opportunity for all children to play and have fun,
regardless of the limits that the world places upon them—
hunger,
racism,
sickness,
religious intolerance,
war,
and the bounds placed on them by their very youth;

the opportunity for all children to be who they are—
natural athletes.

My sincere thanks to all who made this work possible:

my editor and wordsmith—Donna S. Lee;
my friends, critical reviewers, and contributors (and their kids!):
Lisa & Syd Winlock (and Seth & Sammy),
Joyce & Terry Flynn (and Elizabeth, Catherine, & Keenan),
Fran & Andy Edwards (and Shelby, Meagan, & Trent),
Susan & Joel Contreras (and Ironkid Marin),
Bronwyn & Michael Anderson (we're working on it!);
my researcher, reviewer, and friend—Joan Johnson;
and
Campbell Taggart and their Advisory Board:
Virginia Davis,
Liz Appligate, Ph.D.,
Mark Goski,
Debbie Meyers,
Dr. Reginald Washington.

Contents

* R/C BIT is the abbreviation for Rainbo/Colonial Bread Ironkid Triathlon.

Introduction

This is the first triathlon book written for kids. This is the first triathlon book written for parents. This is the first triathlon book written that, if read by both or, better still, read together, can bring kids and parents together to share one of life's most remarkable experiences—playing together.

The book is divided into two sections. The first half of the book is for children ages 7 to 10 (called juniors) and 11 to 14 (called seniors). The last half of the book is for adults—whether junior or senior.

Triathlons for Kids is for any child who wants to learn more about triathlons—how to swim, bike, and run, how to train and race, and lots of other important facts and ideas. The book is a training manual for young triathletes who want to improve or for those who are just getting started. Like the theme song from the Rainbo®/Colonial™ Bread Ironkids Triathlon Series, this book is designed so that "every finisher is a winner." Winners are those who read books to the finish line— the last chapter. Winners study their sport, try new ideas, train with the latest techniques, and talk about it all with their parents.

Triathlons for Kids is also for any parent or other adult who wants to help a child realize their dream. It's a tool that you can use to learn more about triathlon in order to help your child lead an active lifestyle. You'll need to read both sections in the book, not only so you can discuss cross-training with your athlete, but also so you'll know what they are experiencing. Take special care to read the chapter on injuries so you will be able to recognize warning signs and engage in injury prevention. This book is also written for teachers and coaches, as triathlon can easily become a part of your physical education curriculum.

Lastly, *Triathlons for Kids* is for anyone who, like myself, loves to swim, bike, run, and be fit. It is one way to help establish the patterns for both the child and the parent that will guide you toward and through a lifetime of health and fitness.

And to tell you from one tri-kid's experience, here's a letter from my friend, Marin Contreras.

Triathlons....that is a familiar word to me I have grown up around these races. Each summer for the past 6 years, our family has gone to a run, bike, and swim camp at Lake Tahoe, California. As long as I can remember, I have know about Triathlons. I am glad, too, because I think that it is important to exercise and stay healthy! When you do a triathlon you learn about how they work, you also learn responsibilities and discipline because if you don't get yourself and your stuff ready before the race you won't do well. You should also do triathlons for fun. If you come in 1st or even last place as long as you tried really hard and had fun, then you should feel good about yourself.

Triathlons can also help you stay

on a good diet. Because if you are in training you don't eat much junk food or candy. You want to be healthy when you do the triathlons!

Triathlons can also build self esteem. In that last sprint, you have to try to pass the person in front of you. Even if your're shy, when you are sprinting and every body is yelling "Go", "Go", You can't worry about standing out......just do it!

If your're a little nervous about doing a triathlon, take my advice and try one. Because they are a lot of fun! And a wonderful way to stay in shape.

Marin Contreras
age 10

Marin Contreras is an Ironkid. He loves to swim, bike, run and race

Let's Find Out

The sport of triathlon has a very short history. But the three sports that together form triathlon—swimming, cycling, and running—have a very long history.

Let's Find Out about Swimming

We know from very old paintings and writings that people all around the world, from Greece to Japan to America, have been swimming for many thousands of years. They swam both for fun and because they just had to get to places across water. Did you know that the Native Americans held America's first swim competitions?

One of the pioneers of swimming gear was an American named Benjamin Franklin, who also happened to be the person who first harnessed electricity. Franklin's love for swimming led him to create two pieces of triathlon gear: the wetsuit and webbed sandals, which were the first generation of swimming flippers. On top of that, he also designed the first water ski!

There have been many changes in popular swimming styles through the years, as one group of people found out how another group managed to get places in the water more quickly.

The freestyle stroke was brought to England by an Englishman named Trudgen. While on a trip to South America in the 1860s, he saw swimmers doing a windmill-style stroke and noticed that they were very fast. He returned to England and taught the new stroke. Before, the record for 100 yards for men using the breaststroke was 68.5 seconds. In 1902, using Trudgen's stroke, "the crawl," an Australian named Richard Cavill set a world record of 58.6 seconds. The stroke then became known as the Australian crawl.

Improving the Australian crawl, Charles M. Daniels developed the American crawl stroke and set a new world mark in 1906, with a time of 56 seconds for 100 yards. The current world records for 100 *meters* (a meter is a little longer than a yard, so 100 meters equals 109 yards) is 49.4 seconds for men and 54.8 seconds for women.

Rainbo Bread Ironkid Triathlon (R/C BIT) senior division swimmer using the freestyle stroke.

Let's Find Out about Bicycling

The history of bicycling began in 1790, when Frenchman M. de Sivrac built a two-wheeled vehicle. However, this early bicycle didn't have pedals, so the riders had to push the ground with their feet to move forward. This problem kept the bike from becoming very popular.

In 1818, a German named Baron Karl von Drais invented a "hobby horse," a huge two-wheeled machine. The hobby horse was very heavy and made almost entirely of wood—wooden wheels, wooden frame, wooden seat. There were only two problems with this early bike—there were no pedals and no way to steer it. Still, these early types of bicycles were the first inventions to give people transportation beyond the horse and wagon.

On July 27, 1789, a French newspaper first made up the word "bicycle." The newspaper took the word "cycle," which means circle, and added the prefix "bi-," or two. Therefore, a bicycle is a machine with two circles. They used the prefix "tri-," or three, for the first tricycle designed that same year.

The bicycle improved and more people began to ride it. In 1834, a blacksmith attached a rope and connecting rods to a wheel with a pedal. That same year, the gear shift was designed. By 1835, a version with foot pedals on the front wheel was made. Still, by the mid 1800s, the average bicycle cost $100 to $300 (which in today's dollars is over $3,000) and weighed about 60 pounds.

In 1888, the first air-filled tire was designed by J. B. Dunlop, an Irish veterinary surgeon. The development of the air-filled tires transformed the bicycle from a curiosity machine into a true form of transportation and, even more, into a vehicle for competition.

The first official bicycle race in America was held in 1878. Won by Will Pitman, he wheeled his heavy bike over the one-mile course in three minutes and 57 seconds. By 1895, there were over 600 professional bicycle racers in the United States alone and more than that in Europe. However, bicycle racing lost popularity with the invention of the automobile, and America's interest turned to car racing instead.

Let's Find Out about Running

The history of competitive running starts with written records of the single event held in the Olympic Games in 776 B.C. in Olympia, Greece. The event was a 200-yard race for men called "the stade" (our modern word stadium comes from this word) Fifty years later, the double-stade or 400-yard event was started and still later a distance race of about three miles was added.

The modern Olympics were revived in Greece in 1896, and the men's marathon became one of the events. The length of a marathon (26.2 miles or 42.2 kilometers) is the same distance that a Greek soldier ran to get to Athens in order to tell the news of the victory of the Greeks over the Persians more than 2,000 years ago.

The Games include several dozen other sports, but track and field events are still the backbone of the competition. The Olympic decathlon is a multi-skill event, just like triathlon is. But the decathlon can be an even more intense race, because it is made up of *10* events that take place over two *days* of competition.

Let's Find Out about Triathlon

The history of triathlon is almost 20 years long. The speed and spread of its popularity around the world has been amazing. The first known swim-bike-run triathlons were held in San Diego, California, starting in 1974. Other triathlons, consisting of different sports—like Sacramento's Great Race, a run-bike-kayak event—were also becoming popular activities for individuals and relay teams at that time.

In San Diego, these first races were part of weekly training workouts sponsored by a running club and held on summer evenings. A navy officer by the name of John Collins, who had participated in those early low-key events, took the idea to Hawaii. He challenged all of his friends to an "Iron Man"! His race joined three separate Hawaiian races together—the Waikiki Rough Water Swim (2.4 miles), the Around-Oahu Bike Ride (112 miles), and the Honolulu Marathon (26.2 miles)—all in *one* day!

Collins' first unified triathlon was held in 1978, when 12 men completed the race. The following year, one woman and 13 men finished. In 1980, ABC television broadcast the event. By 1985, the Bud Light Ironman World Triathlon, as the race was then named, had over a thousand entries. A great book to read about this is *IRONWILL*, by Mike Plant.

There have been (and will be) a number of important firsts for the sport of triathlon:

1979 • *Sports Illustrated* article on the Ironman

1980 • Ironman televised by ABC "Wide World of Sports"

1981 • *Triathlon Magazine* first published (known today as *Triathlete Magazine*)

1982 • First book written on triathlons: *Triathlon, A Triple Fitness Sport,* by Sally Edwards
• Bud Light United States Triathlon Series' first race
• Nice (France) Triathlon—first professional international triathlon

1985 • Rainbo®/Colonial™ Bread IronkidsTriathlon Series' first race

1990 • Danskin Women's Triathlon Series' first race
• Ironman World Triathlon Series launched with five races on five continents

1991 • IOC (International Olympic Committee recognizes triathlon as an "official sport")

The theme of the R/C BIT series is "Every finisher is a winner."

Let's Find Out about Triathlons for Kids

There are many kids' triathlons, but the biggest are those of the Rainbo®/Colonial™ Bread Ironkids Triathlon Series, which began in 1985. The Rainbo®/Colonial™ Bread Ironkids is more than just a series of races—it is a complete program consisting of the following:

*Rainbo®/Colonial™ Bread Ironkids Club: The club provides detailed race information, a newsletter, tips, a poster, a cassette, and other membership privileges.

*School Program: This consists of five educational units for teachers to use as classroom materials to help teach children nutrition and fitness habits.

*Races: Children can compete and qualify for the national championships in races that are held in over 20 cities in the United States. All of the races are fund-raisers for local charities.

These events are divided into two levels:

Rainbo®/Colonial™ Bread IronkidsTriathlon Distances

		Event Lengths	
Ages	Swim	Bike	Run
Juniors:			
7-10 years	100 meters	5k (3.1 miles)	1k (.6 miles)
Seniors :			
11-14 years	200 meters	10k (6.2 miles)	2k (1.2 miles)

These events are owned and operated by Campbell Taggart, Inc. or its affiliates or their licensees. All rights reserved.

The Rainbo®/Colonial™ Bread Ironkids Triathlon is a way for kids to stay physically fit and have fun at the same time. (See the Appendix for more information.) The theme of the event is "Every Finisher is a Winner," and the emphasis is on winning by setting personal goals and accomplishing them, instead of winning by beating everyone else in the race.

Let's Talk

A Primer of Triathlon Terms

There are a number of terms that you need to know to speak the triathlon language. Let's find out how many of the words of the sport you already know. Check your answers with the "ABC's of Triathlon" or with the answer key that follows.

Triathlon Matching Words Game

_____1.	Tri-Bars	A.	To train hard
_____2.	Triathlete	B.	Aero-bars
_____3.	Hammer	C.	Two-event sport
_____4.	Triathlon	D.	Riding in the slipstream
_____5.	Pulse	E.	Bike-to-run or Swim-to-run
_____6.	Transition	F.	Heart rate
_____7.	Drafting	G.	A heat
_____8.	Bi-Sport	H.	Three-sport athlete

_____9. Cross-Training | I. Doing workouts in more than one sport

_____10. Lap | J. Freestyle stroke

_____11. Front Crawl | K. Two lengths

_____12. Wave | L. Three-event sport

ABC's of Triathlon

AERO-BARS. Handlebars that allow the rider to stretch forward to assume a lower profile while cycling. This keeps cyclists bodies from blocking so much wind and slowing them down. aero-bars are also known as "tri-bars."

BIATHLON. A sport that connects two different sports together. Winter biathlon is made up of cross-country skiing and shooting a rifle while summer biathlon is made up of running and shooting a rifle.

CONDITIONING. A program of physical fitness.

DRAFTING. *a.* This happens when one cyclist rides closely behind another cyclist, using the cyclist in front to block the wind. This is against the rules in triathlon, since it gives the person in back a big advantage. *b.* When someone swims directly behind another person, as closely as possible without touching; it saves energy.

ENDURANCE. When you are able to keep on exercising even when you're tired.

FLEXIBILITY. How far your body is able to stretch in different directions. If you can touch your nose with your toes, *that's* flexible!

The correct answers to the Triathlon Matching Word Game:

1.B 2.H 3.A 4.L 5.F 6.E 7.D 8.C 9.I 10.K 11.J 12.G

GASTROCENEMIUS. The muscle in the back of your lower leg. It's an important muscle to stretch before cycling or running.

HAMMER. An intense workout where you hardly rest at all. Bicycle workouts are often like this.

ITU. The group that makes the rules for triathlon for the entire world—the International Triathlon Union. Tri-Fed/USA is a member of the ITU.

JOGGING. A slow, easy way to run.

KILOMETER. A metric measurement of length that equals .62 miles (a little more than 1/2 a mile).

LAP. Two lengths of the pool—down and back.

MARATHON. A run that is always 26.2 miles long.

NUTRITION. All the ideas behind which foods are good for your body and which ones aren't. Getting a balanced diet that includes lots of fresh food makes good nutritional sense!

OLYMPICS. Held every four years, this is the international competition that determines the best women and men in the world in hundreds of different sports.

PULSE. How fast your heart is beating. It is a way to measure how hard your heart is working to move blood throughout your body.

QUADRICEPS. The muscles on the upper front part of your leg. These are important muscles to stretch before you swim or bike.

RESPIRATION. Breathing—taking in oxygen that the body uses and breathing out carbon dioxide that the body is done with.

SPRINT DISTANCE. A triathlon consisting of a 1/2 mile swim, a 12.5 mile bike and a 3.1 mile run. The "international" or "Olympic distance" is nearly twice this long and consists of a 1,500-meter swim, a 40k bike, and a 10k run.

A young triathlete adding a T-shirt and race number in the swim-to-bike transition area.

TRANSITION. The change-overs between the three sports that happen during a triathlon. For example, between the swim and run is the swim-to-run transition.

UNBELIEVABLE. How you'll feel when you finish a triathlon!

VELOCITY. Speed.

WAVE. A group of triathletes, divided by age or skill, who start a race at the same time and compete together.

XERIC. Dry. Your body becomes this way when you exercise and don't drink enough fluids.

YARDAGE. The distance you cover, measured in yards.

ZIG-ZAG. A sharp turn away from a straight line. You don't want to zig-zag when you run or bike.

Exercise and *training* are the last two words whose meaning and differences you'll need to understand.

You may think of the terms *exercise* and *training* as the same—they are not. *Exercise* is moving—it doesn't matter what the movement is, only that you are moving and, hopefully, enjoy the movement. *Training* means planned exercise—it has a purpose. You train to achieve something, like a goal. In triathlon training, we have a purpose, so we don't just exercise.

4

Let's Think

Heroines and Heroes

I'll bet you have some triathletes that you admire. That's good, because they are examples of what you can become someday if you try. If you are a girl, you probably admire Erin Baker or Paula Newby-Fraser. If you are a boy, you might look up to Dave Scott and Scott Molina. Hopefully, you respect both the women and men pros, because what sex they are shouldn't matter—all of their accomplishments are awesome.

What is most important is that you know that it doesn't really matter what the pros eat or how many yards they swim or who their sponsor is—what really matters is that you learn from their experiences and become a better athlete and a better human being. That's the real reason to pay attention to some-one. So, admire and respect them and imagine that, someday, you can do what they do.

Making Promises to Yourself

For you to be successful, there are a few promises that you need to make with yourself. If you say yes to the following statements, your chances of reaching your goals are very good:

SELF-PROMISES

(check one)

<u>Yes</u> <u>No</u>

- I need to warm up first to get my muscles ready for a workout.

—— ——

- It's OK to walk, slow down, or stop when I am tired.

—— ——

- I will always encourage other kids, not put them down.

—— ——

- It's best to talk while I train, because it means that I still have enough air to breathe and am not over-working myself.

—— ——

- I know that the better my equipment—running shoes, bike equipment, and swimming gear— the safer I will be and the more fun I will have.

—— ——

- The most important part of training is safety—to ride carefully, to slow up or stop exercising if I feel a pain—safety comes before anything else.

—— ——

- Training isn't always easy, but it is fun. My goal is to make it both easy and fun, as often as I can.

—— ——

- I know that there are going to be some problems—it's my job to have as few as possible.

—— ——

Triathletic kids have different goals and dreams of finishing, but most of all they want to have fun.

- I want to know as much as I possibly can about the sport of triathlon, so I will ask lots of questions, read, and learn by participating in the sport.

- I am responsible for demanding that other kids I am with also follow the rules of safety.

Setting Your Goals

Goals have to do with accomplishing something for yourself. What do you really want—to make your family proud or to finish the whole race without stopping or to enjoy the feeling after it is all over? If you can answer these questions, you can probably figure out what it is that you want from triathlon. Everyone has different goals, so you'll have to write out your own in this book, now!

1) How do you want to feel at the start of a race?

*Answer:*_____

_____

_____

_____

2) Is your finish time or your finish place more important, and why?

*Answer:*_____

_____

_____

_____

3) Why do you want to enter a triathlon or train for one?

*Answer:*_____

_____

_____

_____

4) Is it important what your parent(s) think about your performance, and why?

*Answer:*_____

_____

_____

5) What happens to you if you can't finish?

*Answer:*_____

_____

_____

_____

Now that you have answered these five questions, you can start putting together your goal—what it is that you really want to accomplish by participating in a cross-training sport.

Your Parents

You need to tell your parents what you are doing. Parents always have thoughts about what you do, and they can be very helpful and supportive. Ask them to read this book. Ask them if they would like to help you train or train for a triathlon themselves.

Keep your parents informed. You need to let them know about how your training program is going. Show them what you are doing—show them your training program, the tests you will take from this book, the Triathlon Log that you will be keeping, the gear you use, everything.

Keep your teachers informed. Show them the same things you showed your parents. Suggest that they add triathlon to your physical education program, and show them this book.

Most of all, if you have some problems—a pain or a problem with your training partner or if you need equipment—share that with your parents. They want to know. They need to know.

5

Let's Prepare

Swim-Bike-Run are the BEST

There are lots of sports to play, from team sports such as soccer, softball, volleyball, and basketball, to individual sports such as tennis and skiing. As important for developing athletic skills as playing all different kinds of sports is, the three sports that together make up triathlon are the three best for getting your heart and other muscles fit and firm.

The Starting Point

Everything begins with a starting point—that's where you are right now. In fitness training, there is actually a way to measure your starting point. Exercise physiologists, professionals who have measured the fitness levels of thousands of kids, have ways of measuring your general fitness level. The President's Physical Fitness Test, which you may have taken in school, is an example of this.

The measurement of your conditioning is called cardiorespiratory fitness, or the heart's (cardio) and the lungs' (respiratory) ability to exercise. You may have heard of aerobic fitness—cardiorespiratory fitness is the same thing. It is your body's ability to swim, bike, run, and do other activities over a long period of time.

The Resting Heart Rate Test

There is an easy way to measure your fitness. We know that heart rate, or the number of times a heart beats in a given period, is one of the best measurements of your cardiorespiratory fitness level.

First, let's measure your "resting heart rate," or how many beats per minute your heart makes when you are still. You will need a watch that measures seconds to do this. Sit for five minutes—quietly. Then take your pulse by placing three fingers on the artery located just to the side of the middle of your neck. You will feel a very strong pulse when you press gently against this spot on either side of your neck. Count the number of heartbeats in six seconds. Next, add a zero to the end of this number. That is the number of beats per minute, your resting heart rate.

Let's say that in six seconds you counted seven beats. You add a zero after the seven, and you have the number 70. This means that your heart rate is 70 beats per minute.

You need to perform this test three times (once a day for three days) and fill in the blanks:

Resting Heart Rate Score

	Number of Beats in Six Seconds	+ a Zero =		
Test #1	_____	+	0	= _____beats/minute
Test #2	_____	+	0	= _____beats/minute
Test #3	_____	+	0	= _____beats/minute

This number can change depending on a number of things: if you didn't sleep well at night, if you have a cold, if you have had a rough day emotionally, if it is hot/cold out, or if you have eaten or exercised recently. So, don't be surprised if it isn't the same every time.

Target Heart Rate

In triathlon your training goal will be to keep your heart rate within the bull's eye area of the target. This means that there are certain heart rate levels, called "target heart rates," that you want to be at when you work out.

The target heart rate depends on your age and is a fun math problem to solve. Here is the formula:

Low target heart rate:

220 - _____ = _____ x .70 = _____beats per minute
      your age

High target heart rate:

220 - _____ = _____ x .85 = _____beats per minute
      your age

If you don't want to do the math, here are the basic target ranges for each of your ages:

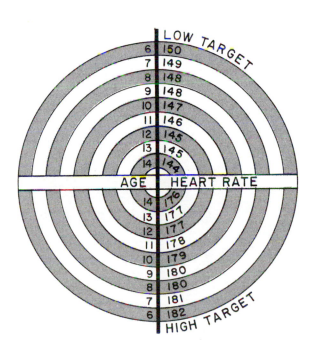

How to Use the Target Heart Rate

After you stop exercising, measure your heart rate for six seconds, just like we did to find the resting heart rate. Add a zero to the number that you counted to find the number of beats per minute that your heart is beating. That number needs to be within the target heart rate zone.

Let's say you are an 8 year-old. Using the chart, the highest rate that your heart should beat to be in the target range is 180 beats, or a count of 18 beats in six seconds. The lowest it should be is 148. If your heart rate is higher than 180, you are going too quickly or are pushing yourself too hard. If your heart rate is lower than 148, then you may be going too slowly or too easily. The goal is to keep your heart rate, after you warm up, between 148 and 180 beats per minute to gain the most fitness from your training.

Your target heart rate is just the right speed for helping your heart grow fit and strong. A fit heart means that you can have the energy to swim and bike and run in a race and still finish with enough energy to enjoy the party afterwards!

For every finish, there is a starting point.

6

Let's Go!

Triathlon is a great sport. It's great because it's a fun way to exercise, a fun way to play, and a fun way to travel. The toys of triathlon—the bike, shoes, swim goggles—are neat stuff. It's fun to do with friends or alone. And it's a sport that you get better in each year.

The three sports of triathlon—swim, bike, run—are ones that most of you already know, since they are some of kids' most popular activities. So getting good at triathlon doesn't mean starting from scratch. Instead, by reading this book and working on all three of these separate sports, you are going to be getting better, faster, and more confident. You will be *improving* your skills, endurance, and fitness.

If one of these triple-fitness sports is new, then you do have a new challenge. But that also means that your rewards from training will be even greater, so get ready, and let's go!

Stretching and Warm Up

Stretching is like a "wake-up" call for your body—it is a chance for all the different parts, such as your muscles and joints, to start working by themselves before the whole body has to move somewhere.

Before and after you swim, bike, or run, you should

spend two to five minutes stretching. When you stretch, don't bounce. Never stretch to the point where it hurts; there should only be a mild feeling of pulling on the muscle. Hold each stretch for 15 to 30 seconds and repeat them several times. See on the next page six good stretches.

The next-best form of stretching is to do your exact workout activity in a very slow and relaxed way. "Stretch-out" in the pool for several laps before you begin your workout. "Stretch-out" on the bike by riding slowly and easily before you start to hammer. "Stretch-out" on the run by walking before you jog and jogging before you run.

Pacing is Critical

The term *pacing* is defined by Webster's Dictionary as "setting or regulating the rate of speed." Pacing means that you go at an even speed for the entire length of the event. If you are going to ride your bike five miles, then you would ride at the same speed over the entire five miles.

Most kids take off at the speed of light when the starter sends them. But *you* are going to start at the same speed that you finish. That's what your heroines and heroes all do, and it is called "even pacing." The champs know that speed is not what wins races. What wins races is going as fast as you can, but *at an even speed.*

Heat and Cold, Light and Dark

There are natural dangers that you have to beware of to participate safely in triathlon. On a hot, humid day, your body may not be able to cope with the temperatures, and you can experience heatstroke. Or a windy winter day can be so cold that the heat drains away from your body faster than you can make it, and you may suffer from frostbite or frozen skin. You can find out what the day's weather will be like by checking your local newspaper or calling the weather report number which should be listed in your phone book.

You also need to be visible. Drivers need to know that you are on your bike, lifeguards need to see that you are swimming, and other people should be aware of you when you are running.

Stay "light" in the dark. Don't go out in the dark at all, if

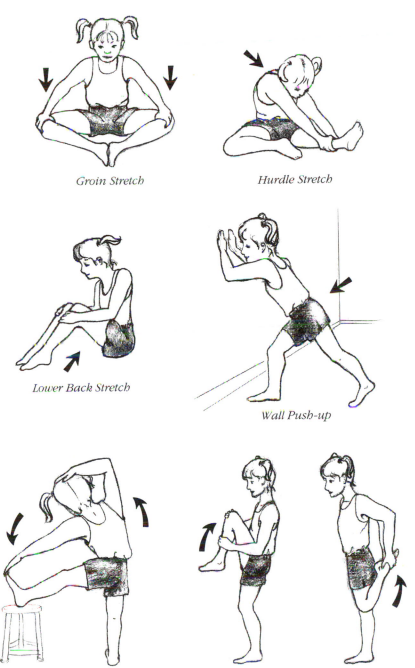

Groin Stretch

Hurdle Stretch

Lower Back Stretch

Wall Push-up

Hamstring Stretch

Leg Puller Stretches

THE BASIC SEVEN. Stretches that prepare you for your workout.

you can help it. If you have to go out at night, wear reflective gear, use a flashlight, and never go alone.

A Training Partner

It's a great idea to team up with a friend who also wants to be a triathlete. If you can get a group of kids your age together, a whole bunch of training buddies, better still.

There are two main reasons for training partners. The first is that they encourage you and keep you company both on good days, when both of you feel like training, and on bad ones, when one of you might not. Let's say that you don't feel like swimming on a certain day. If you know that your partner is going to be there to meet you though, you will still go so that you won't disappoint them. Or, if they are feeling down, they will still show up to meet you. The only time that you won't train then is when you both don't want to. That means that three out of four times you are supposed to train, you *will* train. So, since the chances are much greater that you will work out if you have a partner, get a buddy, make a pact, and tri-train!

The other reason to train with a partner is in case any problems come up. For example, if one of you were to get hurt while training, the other could go get help. So it's very important to have a training buddy, but if you can't find a partner, start training anyway. Soon enough, one of the kids you know will find out what you are doing and want to join in on the fun.

Training partners can easily become your best friend.

Your Training Log

It's going to help a lot if you write down how you are doing and what you are thinking and feeling as you train. That is the purpose of the Triathlon Log—it is a journal that belongs to you and is only for you and those you allow to read it. Write in it every day. Write down your workouts, your target heart rates, the weather, and, of course, what you did or didn't do that day.

If you don't keep a log, you tend to forget.

And by writing all this down, you can also see how much better you get as the weeks go by.

Here is a sample page like the one you might keep. Notice that there is a lot of information in it other than about tri-training. Your Triathlon Log, like your journal, is a way that years from now you'll know how you felt, what you did, and who you enjoyed being with.

You can make your own Triathlon Log by making copies from this book. Or, you can write away and you or your parents can send a check for $7.95 (includes shipping and handling charges) for a copy of the whole book. The Triathlon Log also has tips, graphs to follow your training, and additional information. Order them from:

FLEET FEET PRESS
2408 "J" Street
Sacramento, CA 95816
(916) 442-3338

Courses

I have found that if I set up several different courses to work out on, my workouts are easier to do because I don't get bored. You can't really set up a course in a swimming pool, though, so with swimming you can only vary the number of laps. (Unless, of course, there is a lake or other body of water nearby where adults can watch you, then you can design away!)

On the bike, I like to plan out lots of different routes for my workouts. I suggest that you set up separate one-mile, five-mile and 10-mile bike courses. If you have a bike trail nearby, it will usually be marked with mileage markers, so it'll be easy to know your distances. Or you can get a friend with a cyclometer, a device that measures distance while on the bike, and have them ride and measure it with you. You can also measure the length of your workouts by timing them, using time instead of distance as your measure.

When running, I like to run around things—around the park, around the outside of a softball or soccer field, around the track at the school, or around the block. If there is a trail nearby, I like to run there, too, so that I don't always run on asphalt. I *only* run on trails, though, when my training partner is with me, so I have some company if I end up a long way away from home. Again, you can run by distance, such as on marked trails, or by timing yourself. Whichever way you measure your workouts, make sure to do it the same way each time, so you can compare!

On different days you are going to feel differently about training on your courses. Some days you may be slower and other days faster and not really know why. That's the way all of us feel. Some days you may want to train at the top of your target heart rate range and other days at the bottom. These are called "hard" and "easy" days, and both are part of your training program.

You should now know where you are—the starting point—so...

Let's Go!

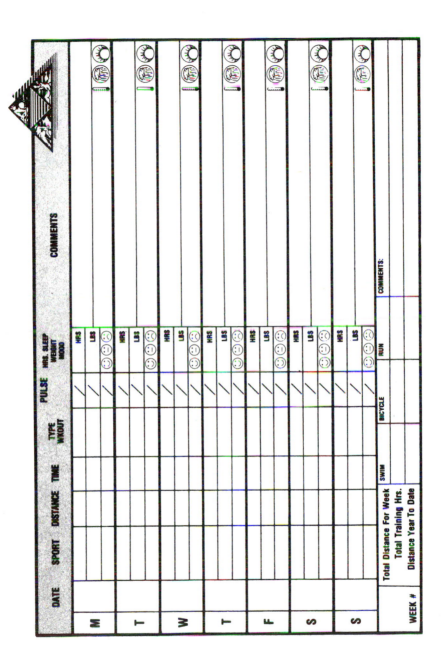

Note: The Triathlon Log is available from FLEET FEET PRESS, 2408 "J" Street, Sacramento, CA 95816 for $7.95.

DATE		SPORT	DISTANCE	TIME	TYPE WKOUT	PULSE	HRS SLEEP / LBS WEIGHT / MOOD	COMMENTS
M	3/5	Swim		10 mins	Fun	15/10	8 HRS / 76 LBS / ⊗ ☹	Today was my first day with my new swim club
T	3/6						HRS / LBS / ☹	
W	3/7	Bike		20 min.	EASY	70/100	HRS / LBS / ⊗ ☹	Rode with Sara on our 3 mile course in the neighborhood
T	3/8						HRS / LBS / ☹	
F	3/9	Run		15 mins	non-stop		HRS / LBS / ⊗ ☹	Ran 4 times around the track at the school with my mom — she did more
S	3/10						HRS / LBS / ☹	Went on family weekend trip
S	3/11						HRS / LBS / ☹	Camped out, but it was cold

	SWIM	BICYCLE	RUN	COMMENTS:
Total Distance For Week				
Total Training Hrs.				
Distance Year To Date				

WEEK #

7

Swim!

To begin, you must know how to swim the freestyle stroke for at least one length of a pool. If you can't do this yet, don't worry. The freestyle stroke is easy to learn—you can take classes or have someone you know teach you the basics.

What You Will Need

Except for possible pool fees, swimming is a cheap sport. All you need are a suit, goggles, and a cap, which together can cost as little as $20 to $30.

In choosing goggles, hold a pair up to your eyes and push on them. If they are the right fit, they will hold for several seconds before falling off. If you don't have any luck with one style of goggle, try others—there are many different brands and styles of goggles to choose from.

If your goggles fog, there are defogging solutions that you can use. Or you can wash the inside with soap, rinse them in water, and add a few drops of saliva to the inside of the goggles, and you may not need to buy any defogger. Also, most goggles leak until you take the time to tighten or loosen them and make them fit you.

In picking a suit, get one that fits skintight so that you will be faster in the water. Rinse it out after *every* swim, to keep it clean and you healthy.

A swim cap is not required, but it helps to protect your hair from the chemicals in the pool (like goggles protect your eyes). Pick a brightly colored cap—you want lifeguards to be able to see you when you swim.

Where Can You Train?

You need to find a swimming pool with open swim hours or sign up for a swim class. Check local schools—they might have a pool that they allow students to use. Recreation districts have swimming pools, so do the YMCA/YWCA and private clubs. These places also often have groups of swimmers who train together—ask them if you can join up, too. It's more fun to train with others, and it is also a very good way to make friends.

Stroke Mechanics

The freestyle is the fastest swimming stroke and is the only one that should be used in triathlons, if you can help it. The stroke is made up of upper and lower body motions that are linked together: the underwater armstroke, the above-water armstroke, the kick, correct body positioning, and breathing.

The Underwater Armstroke

1. Pull pattern is a long "S" shape.
2. Elbow is bent up to 90 degrees.
3. Elbow is high, not dropped.
4. Arm is extended forward for longest pull.
5. Hand moves faster from the beginning to the end of the pull.
6. The body rolls from side to side as the arm is pulled in "S" shape.
7. Palm is flat with fingers pointed and close together.

THE UNDERWATER ARMSTROKE
The pull pattern is a long "S" shape.

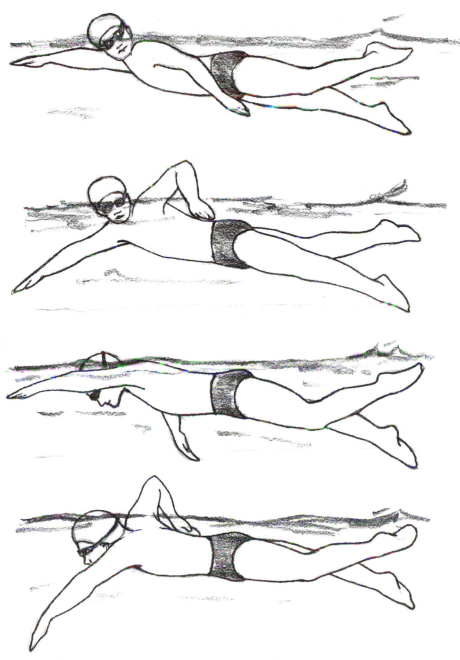

FREESTYLE STROKE. Look at the circular armstroke, the flutter-kick leg action, and breathing in and out with the head turned.

The Above-water Armstroke

1. When the arm is above the water, swing it forward, relaxed.
2. Hand enters the water thumb first, little finger last, palm outward.
3. Hand leaves the water little finger first, thumb last.

The Two-beat Flutter Kick

1. Ankles are relaxed.
2. Kicks are small with heels breaking the surface.
3. Knee is straight on the upbeat.
4. Knee is bent slightly on the downbeat.
5. Toes are pointed, use the entire leg from the hip to the toes.
6. Kick two times for each two arm circles.

Body Positioning

1. Water crosses the face at the hairline.
2. Arms remain opposite each other.
3. Body is in a straight line.
4. Body rolls from side to side as one unit.
5. Eyes look forward and downward.

Breathing

1. Head is rolled, not lifted, to the side for breathing in.
2. Face is looking at the bottom of the pool when you breathe out.
3. Breathe out *all* of your air just as your head rolls outward.

Interval Training

Interval training is about working out at different amounts of effort or intensity, instead of just coasting along at an even level of effort. By exercising really hard for a little while, then less hard, then more hard again, you condition your body's muscles and increase your endurance (the amount of time you can exercise without stopping) very quickly.

Intervals are the method of training used by competitive swimmers. In the beginning, the way we talk about intervals can be sort of complicated to understand, so don't expect to get the whole idea just from reading this, if you've never heard about intervals before. After you get more involved in swim-

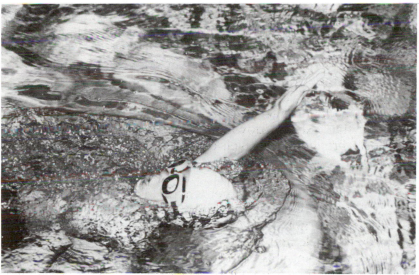

Freestyle swim stroke—notice how the swimmer rolls on to their side as they breathe.

ming, this will make more sense. For now, the basic idea is that intervals or "repeats" are set distances that are repeated, with a set amount of rest between each.

An example of an interval set is to swim three different lengths of 50 yards, with 30 seconds rest between each set. This interval set is written as follows:

3 x 50 yd/30 sec

Another way that intervals are repeated is on the "out time" or the time that you depart from the pool wall. The swim time plus the rest time combine to a total time that then represents the time at which you leave for the next interval. For example, if you swim 50 yards three times and leave on (@ means "on") the 55 seconds, it is written as follows:

3 x 50/yd @ 55 sec

Answers to Common Problems:

Problem: My eyes hurt.
Solution: Your goggles are leaking, and the chemicals in the pool water are causing eye aches. Don't rub your eyes or

use eye wash—wash them out with tap water. And either tighten your goggles until they fit or buy new ones.

Problem: My body wiggles from side to side as I swim.

Solution: You may be swinging your arms to the side when they are above the water. You may be "crossing-over" or making your hand enter the water past the midline (an imaginary line that extends down the middle of your body—from your feet, through your navel, through the center of your head forward).

Problem: I swallow water when I take a breath.

Solution: Blow all of your air out just as your face rolls out of the water, not after your face is in the open air. You now are ready to inhale and have enough time to do so. To test and see if you are doing this, stand sideways to a mirror, bending at the waist. Then practice your strokes to see if you are breathing at the right times. You *shouldn't* see yourself breathing out when you turn your head to face the mirror.

Problem: My ears ache.

Solution: This is called "swimmer's ear" and is a rash-like inflammation of the ear canal caused by water. Dry out your ears after swimming and put in ear drops. You can buy a pair of good-fitting ear plugs from an ear doctor or drug store.

Problem: I have a dull aching pain in my shoulders.

Solution: This is common for the first few weeks of training, and it should go away. If it doesn't, you might have tendinitis or inflamed tendons and ligaments in the shoulder joint. If it continues, you must get help from your doctor. You might have to change the way you make your stroke or change to a different stroke from freestyle.

Problem: I bob up and down.

Solution: Your "S" shaped curve is off track. Look at your hand and make sure that it is facing at the best angle to push water backward as you pull and move forward.

8

Bike!

Cycling is a great sport, and more and more kids are finding they have the talent and skills for it. Many kids find it to be their favorite sport of all and the easiest part of a triathlon, since the distance goes by quickly and the bike helps with the work!

Get to know your bike. Get to know it really well, like a friend and a training partner. Get to know when it has mechanical problems. Get to know how to keep it under control when you are on the edge—of a turn or of a disaster. Get to know it so you can ride your best.

To get to know your bike that well, you must start by knowing about all of the following things.

Start with the Right Bike

The right bike is one that fits you and meets your needs. If you need a bike to ride to school, a bike to train on, a bike to ride in a triathlon, a bike that can go almost anywhere, you need a cross between a beach cruiser, a roadster, a city bike, a BMX, a sport bike, a mountain bike, a touring bike, and a racing bike.

There aren't any such amazing combination bikes, though, so it is best to decide on your needs and then make sure that whatever bike you choose fits. A bike that's too big—

Light Roadster

Heavy Roadster

Commuter/City Bikes

Beach Cruiser

Touring Bikes

Sport Touring Bikes

Touring Mountainbikes

Sport Mountainbikes

Competition Mountainbikes

Sports Bikes

Road Racing Bikes

Track Bikes

that you can "grow into"—will be very hard to get on and off of safely. All bikes have room to grow built into them, and you can make them fit by adjusting the handlebars and seat. You are looking for a bike that fits you *now*, is light, and rolls easily.

Really, almost any old bike can get you through your first few triathlons, and no one is going to keep you from competing (or winning!) just because your bike isn't this year's model. But if you do want to be highly competitive, you should have the best bike you can afford. And don't expect your bike to be cheap because it is small—good ones for kids cost the same as adult bikes.

Fit the bike to you, not you to the bike. Straddle the top tube (the horizontal bar that goes from the seat to the handlebars) and make sure that you can stand flat-footed and not touch the top tube. Test-ride the bike before you buy it. If you are looking at several bikes that are about the same price, ride each one, and buy the one that feels most comfortable and easy to ride.

A three-speed rear hub bicycle, with caliper brakes front and rear, might be the starter bike for you, if you are 9 years old or younger. For kids older than that, a 10-speed is best. Here's a chart to help you figure out exactly what size bike frame you will need:

Triathlons for Kids
BICYCLE FRAME SIZES

Your Approximate Height	Your Bike Frame Size	
(Feet/inches)	(inches)	(cm)
4'1"-4'3"	12-12.5	30.5-31.8
4'3"-4'5"	13-13.5	33.0-34.3
4'5"-4'7"	14-14.5	35.6-36.8
4'7"-4'9"	15-15.5	38.1-39.4
4'9"-4'11"	16-16.5	40.6-41.9
4'11"-5'1"	17-17.5	43.2-44.5
5'1"-5'3"	18-18.5	45.7-47.0
5'3"-5'5"	19-19.5	48.3-49.5
5'5"-5'7"	20-20.5	50.8-52.1
5'7"-5'9"	21-21.5	53.3-54.6

Go ahead and buy all the accessories: pump, lock, helmet, water bottles and cages for them, and a pair of bike shorts, at the same time as you buy the bike; it'll save you trouble later.

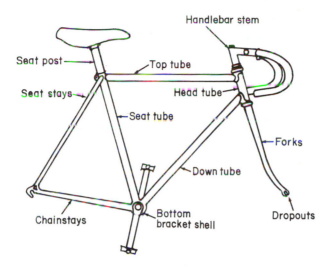

THE BIKE FRAME. *There are seven different tubes on a 10-speed: Head tube, seat tube, down tube, top tube, seat stays, chainstays, forks.*

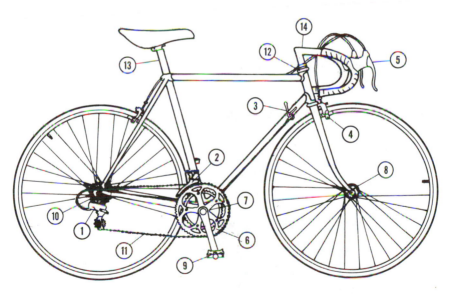

1. *Rear derailleur*	6. *Crank set*	11. *Chain*
2. *Front derailleur*	7. *Bottom bracket*	12. *Headset*
3. *Shift lever*	8. *Hub*	13. *Seat post*
4. *Caliper brake*	9. *Pedal*	14. *Handlebar*
5. *Brake lever*	10. *Freewheel*	*Stem*

BIKE COMPONENTS. *The different parts that attach to the frame.*

What If You Can't Afford a Bike?

Bikes are definitely expensive, but you need one to do a triathlon. If you are having trouble buying one, here are some ideas that might help you and a bike come together:

1. Earn—You can provide your family or your friends' families a service, like mowing lawns or baby-sitting, in order to earn the money to buy your own bike.

2. Borrow—If someone you know has a bike they are not using, or have outgrown, you might ask if they would loan it to you.

3. Win—Service clubs such as the Kiwanis or the Rotary Club often make gifts of bikes to kids who want to participate in sports.

The One-Minute Helmet Lesson

You *must* use a helmet anytime you ride a bicycle.

It must meet the helmet standards set by either one of two organizations—Snell or ANSI. The helmets that these groups approve have stickers on them to show that they meet safety standards.

Buy white or yellow helmets for best visibility.

If you crash, replace the helmet. Replace it if anything cracks or breaks on it, like a strap or buckle. Some companies, like Giro, have a guaranteed free helmet-replacement policy.

Bike accidents are very common and are a major cause of injury to kids. Wearing a helmet can keep you healthy and safe, so always wear one!!

Benjamin Meyers, age 3 with author—helmets are required gear whenever you ride your bike— regardless of age.

Make The Bike Fit You

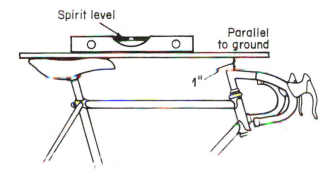

Saddle Level. Parallel to the ground.
Handlebar Height. One inch below the height of your saddle.

Saddle Position. At the 3 o'clock position, the pedal is lined up with the front of your knee.

Make The Bike Fit You

There is no one way to fit a bike to you. You have to try different positions for the saddle height, the handlebar height and length, and the saddle tilt. Here are a few things to remember for getting the correct fit:

- Saddle Height: Should be at a place where your knee is not quite straight at the bottom of the pedal stroke.
- Saddle Level: Parallel to the ground.
- Saddle Position: Move the saddle forward and backward until you find the position where, when your pedal is as far forward as possible (3 o'clock position), the pedal is lined up with the front of your knee.
- Handlebar Stem Length: Depends on the kind of handlebars. If you have dropped bars, when your hands are on the drop with your head up, the end of your nose should line up with the farthest forward position of the bars.
- Handlebar Height: Approximately 1 inch below the height of your saddle.

How to Maintain the Bike

Who should do the maintenance on your bike? If you can and want to learn, read the owner's manual and do it yourself. If you make a mistake, you can always take it to the shop and have them show you the best way to fix the problem.

Here's a quick checklist of the most common problems that can happen with your bike:

- Rattles: Sounds like clicking, rubbing, and rattling are probably from loose parts. Use a wrench, screwdriver or allen key and tighten the problem part.
- Tires: Slow leaks or smooth tread means it's time to fix the tube or replace the tire. Knowing how to pull the tube out, patch it, and put it back together is an important and easy lesson to learn.
- Chain: Keep it clean from road dirt and well-lubricated. If it gets dry, squirt lubricant on the chain, hold a rag against it, and slowly turn the pedals backward.

Here's a list of maintenance that the bike shop should do:

- Broken wheel spokes
- Brake adjustments and brake pads
- Gears that don't shift right
- Frame damage
- Wheel alignment

How to Ride a Bike Safely

You steer the bike, it doesn't steer you.

Beginners think that you sit on the seat, push with the legs, bend the back, and steer with the hands.

Trained cyclists know that you straddle the saddle, spin the pedals, slope the back, and steer by balance.

Here are the most common bicycle-handling practices that you need to follow to ride safely:

- **Partners:** Always try to ride with a buddy. It's safer and more fun.

- **Signaling:** There are three signals for each of the three changes in movement you may make—left, right, and stop. For a right turn, straighten your right arm and point to the right. To indicate that you are stopping, hold up your right arm, bending it down at the elbow. For a left turn, extend your left arm and point to the left. Then you must also follow the correct way of changing lanes. First, look back at the traffic and then, if it is clear, ride to the dotted centerline, keeping your arm out.

- **Hazards:**
  - Driveways: If you are riding out of a driveway, stop at the end of it and look before riding forward.
  - Wrong-way Riding: Ride in the same direction with cars—don't ride towards them. It's the law.
  - Opening Car Doors: A person sitting in a parked car can't see a cyclist, so they might open the door without knowing that you are there. Look for drivers who are about to leave their cars.

-Dogs: Shout in a deep voice, "Go home!" If necessary, get off your bike, keep it in front of the dog, and walk to the other side of the road. Chances are the dog won't follow you.

-Reckless Cyclists: Most can't ride a straight line, so give them a lot of room in front of you—don't "draft."

-Bumps: Roll over bumps, if you can't go around them, by pulling up on the handlebars.

-Shifting Gears: Shift slowly, so you don't pop the chain off the bike.

-Braking: To stop quickly, apply force to both the front and back wheels, so that you don't fly over the handlebars. If the rear wheel goes into a skid, let up on the front brake and transfer your body weight to the rear wheel by sliding your rump backwards off the saddle.

-Sidewalks: Don't ride on them, and don't hop them.

-Intersections: Obey *all* traffic rules, and always yield the right of way to cars. When there is NO TRAFFIC, you can ride through.

-Stop Signs: Always stop completely, putting your foot down on the ground. Look both ways, and, when the roads are clear, ride again. In one triathlon, it was a rule that all the triathletes had to put one foot down at every stop sign. One competitor broke the rule and was not only disqualified, she also lost all of her prize money, because she had finished first!

-Traffic Lights: Obey the color of the light. If the light is turning from green to yellow, always stop.

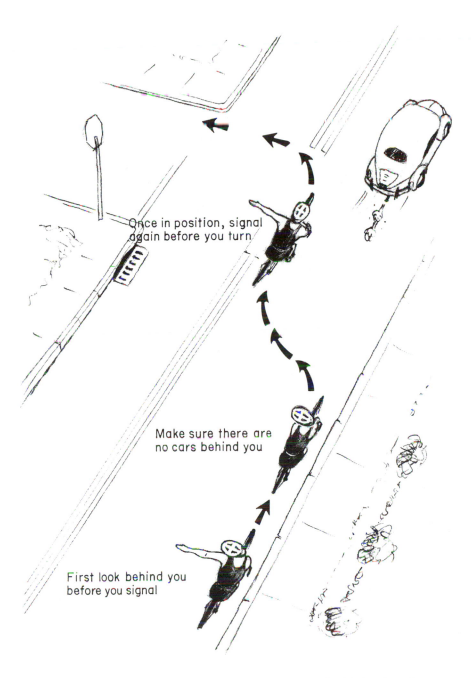

Once in position, signal again before you turn

Make sure there are no cars behind you

First look behind you before you signal

LEFT TURNS ARE THE HARDEST. You must signal twice, look behind, and only turn when there are no cars.

There are 14 unsafe things in this picture. How many of them can you find? Take a pencil and circle the ones that you find. Then turn the book upside down and compare your answers with the correct ones.

9

Run!

Running is a sport that is useful as well as fun. Take Mexico's Tarahumara Indians for an example. For centuries running has been a way of life for them. Living in Mexico's Sierra Madre, a region too rugged even for burros, the Tarahumaras run, rather than walk, for most of their daily movement. Around 1900, one runner carried a message nearly 250 miles, and then returned to his village in five days.

For fun, the Tarahumara tribe plays a kickball game. Using a wooden ball about the size of a softball, the kickball racers may run as many as 100 miles or more and continue without rest for three days and nights.

For these Indian athletes, running long distances is fun.

For you, running can be, too.

Equipment

Starting a running program requires only one piece of equipment—shoes. Today's sneaker manufacturers—Nike, Reebok, Brooks, Saucony—all make running shoes for children. Here are some tips in choosing a pair that will work for you:

- *Buy the right size:* Your parents may want you to "grow into them" and ask that you try shoes that are over-sized. This only leads to foot problems that are not worth the extra few weeks that you can wear too-big shoes.

- *Buy the right style:* Different running shoes are made for different kinds of feet. When your feet strike the ground, they may roll in, roll out, or a combination of these. You may also need a lot of cushioning for a soft ride, or a firm shoe that controls your foot. Buy the shoes that fit your style of running.

- *Buy them for quality, not price:* All of us have budgets, *until* it comes to athletic shoes, then we need to pay for the best that we can buy. It is cheaper to spend $10 more for shoes, than $100 for a doctor's visit.

- *Buy them to run, not play in:* Your running shoes should be used for just that—running. When they are worn out, you can use them for other sports. But until then, only wear them when you work out.

- *Buy them for feel, not fashion:* It doesn't matter what they look like, it only matters what they feel like. Buying shoes that fit is the most important thing, not their color or brand name, and not the celebrity athletes who may also wear them.

- *Buy the best shoe for you:* There is no best shoe for everyone, but there is one for you. Take the time at the store to "test run" at least three or four styles, until you find the best shoe for you, not for someone else. The best shoe provides support, flexibility, and cushioning, and fits your toes, heel, and arches comfortably.

Hot and Cold Running

Dressing for running is easy. Wear whatever you like that you can move around in, and don't wear too much. Remember that your body works like a furnace, not like an air conditioner. As you jog, your temperature rises. The air temperature feels like it is 20 degrees hotter than it was before you started running. In other words, a comfortable 65 degree temperature feels like a hot 85 degrees. This is called the "Twenty Degree Rule."

The Twenty Degree Rule

Rule: The temperature seems to rise by about 20 degrees when you run. Dress knowing that your furnace is going to get that much hotter. Dress in layers so that as you get warmer, you can take off clothes and cool down.

You can run in almost any kind of weather. When it is really hot or really cold, though, you need to be concerned about your clothes, so that you can work out without discomfort.

In hot weather, dress in lightweight clothes, try to run in the shade, and run more slowly. Drink lots of water during the run, as well as before and after. If you overheat, you will feel dizzy or like you have the chills—if this happens, stop and walk. If you fight the heat, *you* lose, not the heat.

In cold weather, dress warmly. Wear a hat and gloves. Wear layers of clothes, like a short-sleeve T-shirt, under a long-sleeve T-shirt, under a sweatshirt or jacket. If the wind is blowing, run with it toward your back when you first start. And don't run too far from home, so that if you get really cold, home will still be nearby.

In rain, wear a windbreaker or nylon jacket, and try to keep as dry as you can. A baseball cap, or any hat with a brim, will keep the water off your face and out of your eyes. Change into dry clothes when you get home.

Safety

There are certain rules of running that you have to follow. Here are a few of them:

- *Always run with someone else.* Whenever you can, run with an adult or a friend. It's not only more fun, it is also safer.

- *Tell someone where you are going.* That is a rule anytime you go anywhere, but especially when running.

- *Run where there are no cars.* Stay away from traffic when you run. Run around a school, through a park, on a track, sidewalk, or bike path, but not in the street.

- *If you must run where there are cars, run towards*

Running can be even more fun when you run with others.

them. If you must run where there are cars, run on the left side of the road, facing them. Car drivers have a hard time seeing you, so always think that they won't.

- *Follow the rules of the road.* Cross streets at crosswalks, and only cross when the signal allows you to do so. Remember to look both ways before you cross.

- *Run the speed you know.* Don't try to run faster than you have ever run before. Don't run farther than you have ever run before. Don't do either without following the first rule—always run with someone else.

Running Style

You know how to run—it's natural, and it's you. But there may be ways you can run easier and faster, if you don't already have a smooth running style. Still, you only want to change your running style if you think that you are developing bad habits—don't just mess around with your natural form for the heck of it. Here is the ideal running form:

Feet (Footplant)
- Foot hits on the heel first.
- Foot strikes, usually on the outside of the heel, and the foot rolls inward.

- Foot pushes off using the toes.
- Heel should strike the ground directly under the hips.
- Feet land quietly; they don't slap the ground.

Legs
- Knees should be directly over the feet when the feet land.
- No knee-lift or back-kick of the foot.
- Leg does not straighten (this can break the leg).
- Run low to the ground, don't bounce.

Arms and Hands
- Hands lightly clenched (like holding a dime between your thumb and forefinger).
- Elbow is bent, but not locked.
- Keep arms low, not swinging high like a boxer's.
- Keep wrists straight, not limp.
- Keep arms shoulder-width apart and don't let them cross your chest.
- Arms swing in rhythm with legs.

Running form like this is what you should practice.

Head and Shoulders

- Head does not tilt—it stays straight.
- Keep your neck, jaw, and shoulders totally relaxed.
- Shoulders are level, parallel to the ground, relaxed, not shrugged.
- Eyes should focus 6 feet out from your feet, not straight down at the ground.

Stomach

- When you breathe "in," your stomach goes out; when you breathe "out," your stomach goes in.
- Breathe regularly, not in short breaths.
- Breathe in through your mouth and nose.

The efficient running style looks like this:

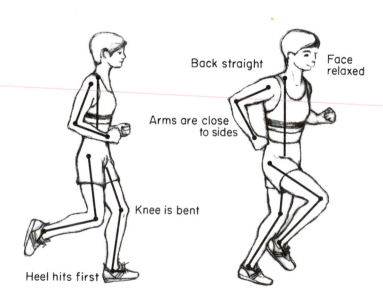

Back straight

Face relaxed

Arms are close to sides

Knee is bent

Heel hits first

Pacing

This is a word that refers to how fast you are running. Most runners find it best to run at an even pace, one that does not change as they go through the length of the race.

You have to *learn* how to pace yourself. At first, you might find that you start to run quickly and then slow down. This is not a good idea, because in a race, dashing past everyone in the beginning doesn't help if you can't last to the end.

So when you run, how quickly you run isn't as important as how evenly paced you run. Do you remember one of the first times you ever ran? Did you run super-fast and then, feeling totally tired, want to quit or walk? Did you feel as if you couldn't run another step?

With even pacing, you won't feel that way. Pacing yourself makes running easy and fun and also makes sure that you get to cross the finish line standing up!

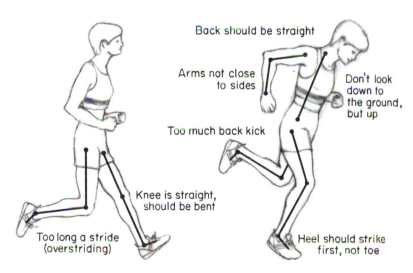

Incorrect Running Form

When you have trained properly, you finish by giving it your "all."

10

Training

Setting up a weekly training program requires you to make some choices and plans. Most importantly, you must decide if you are ready to swim, bike, and run on a regular schedule.

Here are some basic questions and answers about your triathlon training program:

- How many days per week should you train?
                                    Answer: 3-6 days
- How many continuous weeks?
                                    Answer: 4-8 weeks
- How much time per workout?
                                    Answer: From 10-40 minutes
- What distance per workout?
                                    Answer: Train by time, not distance
- How hard should you train?
                Answer: Use your target heart rate (see Chapter 5)

Beat the Clock

There are only two ways of deciding on "how long" you work out—by keeping time or measuring the distance. Swimmers usually count laps, bicyclists log miles on their cyclometers, and runners run by a wristwatch. Athletes always try to find some way of measuring their training sessions, so that they have a way of keeping track of the length of their work-outs.

All the training schedules in this book will be written to beat the clock. That means that we are using time as the way of measuring the length of the workout.

Let's say that you are going to do a 20-minute workout. The workout needs to be divided into three parts: the warm-up, the main set, and the cool down. Follow the 20%-60%-20% method and divide the 20 minutes into three parts: 20 percent or four minutes for your warm-up, 60 percent or 12 minutes for the main set, and 20 percent or four minutes for a cool down.

The entire workout looks like this:

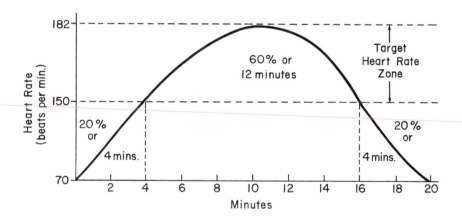

Can you calculate the 20%-60%-20% warm-up, main set, and cool-down for a 30-minute workout? Here's the formula: .20 x 30 = _____ and .60 x 30 = _____.

The main set is 60 percent of your workout time. During this time, you want to train within your target heart rate, as explained in Chapter 5. The warm-up period is the time that you slowly raise your heart rate to the target range, and the cool-down period is the time that you slowly crank back on the pace and your heart rate returns to a near-resting speed.

Climbing the Mountain

As you train through the weeks, you get fitter, and, as you get in better shape, the same workouts become easier. But to keep on getting in better shape, you'll need to keep on training at your target heart rate. So, you will notice that you are going faster and, at the same time, that it is easier. I call this "climbing the mountain," because it reminds me of swimming, cycling, or running to the peak:

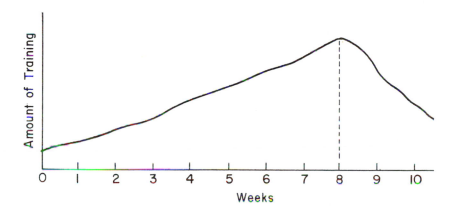

If you decide after eight weeks to cut back on your workouts, you will slide back down the mountain, just like in the drawing here.

What do you do when you reach the peak of the mountain? That's easy: you set new goals, draw new mountains, and start climbing again! In sports training, this is called "building a base." Your first mountain is your base. When you reach the top you have made it to "base camp"—a resting point for the next climb to the next peak.

Sample Training Programs

There is no one right training program for every kid. However, there are some examples of training programs that you can use in planning your own personal one.

It's a good idea to talk to your parents and friends about your training program. They may have some experience and will want to help, and it will give you support just to have them involved.

I have written some training schedules for you to use as examples in making your own. Don't *follow* these—*use* them as guides. These guidelines are written with three things in mind:

- That you are new to all three sports—that you don't have competitive experience in any of them.

- That you don't have any sport that is weaker than any other. These programs are balanced and do not emphasize any weakest sport that you might have. If one or two of your sports skills are weaker than the other(s), you will have to spend more time with the weaker one(s) and less with the stronger one(s) than I have planned here. *Don't* spend most of your time with your favorite or easiest sport. You need to be balanced, good in all three sports, to be a successful triathlete!

And, lastly,

- That you start with three or four workouts per week and can progress to five or six workouts per week.

8 Week Triathlon Training Program
Juniors (age 7-10 years)

Schedule (in Minutes)

WEEK #1

	Swim	Bike	Run
Monday	10	—	—
Tuesday	—	—	—
Wednesday	—	15	—
Thursday	—	—	—
Friday	—	—	10
Saturday	—	—	—
Sunday	—	—	—
Total Minutes	10	15	10 = 35 min.

WEEK #2

	Swim	Bike	Run
Monday	10	—	—
Tuesday	—	—	—
Wednesday	—	—	15
Thursday	—	—	—

Friday	——	20	——
Saturday	——	——	——
Sunday	——	——	——
Total Minutes	10	20	15 = 45 min.

WEEK #3

	Swim	Bike	Run
Monday	15	——	——
Tuesday	——	——	——
Wednesday	——	——	——
Thursday	——	——	15
Friday	——	——	——
Saturday	——	20	——
Sunday	——	——	——
Total Minutes	15	20	15 = 50 min.

WEEK #4

	Swim	Bike	Run
Monday	15	——	——
Tuesday	——	——	——
Wednesday	——	25	——
Thursday	——	——	——
Friday	——	——	20
Saturday	——	——	——
Sunday	——	——	——
Total Minutes	15	25	20 = 60 min.

4 Week Average = 47 minutes per week

WEEK #5

	Swim	Bike	Run
Monday	20	——	——
Tuesday	——	——	——
Wednesday	——	——	20
Thursday	——	——	——
Friday	——	30	——
Saturday	——	——	——
Sunday	——	——	——
Total Minutes	20	30	20 = 70 min.

WEEK #6

	Swim	Bike	Run
Monday	20	——	——
Tuesday	——	——	——
Wednesday	——	20	——
Thursday	——	——	——

	Swim	Bike	Run
Friday	—	—	20
Saturday	—	15	—
Sunday	—	—	—
Total Minutes	20	35	20 = 75 min.

WEEK #7

	Swim	Bike	Run
Monday	25	—	—
Tuesday	—	15	—
Wednesday	—	—	15
Thursday	—	—	—
Friday	—	20	—
Saturday	—	—	10
Sunday	—	—	—
Total Minutes	25	35	25 = 85 min

WEEK #8

	Swim	Bike	Run
Monday	25	—	—
Tuesday	—	20	—
Wednesday	—	—	15
Thursday	—	—	—
Friday	—	20	—
Saturday	—	—	10
Sunday	—	—	—
Total Minutes	25	40	25 = 90 min.

Second 4 Week Average = 80 minutes per week

8 Week Triathlon Training Program
Seniors (age 11-14 years)

Schedule (in Minutes)

WEEK #1

	Swim	Bike	Run
Monday	10	—	—
Tuesday	—	—	—
Wednesday	—	15	—
Thursday	—	—	—
Friday	—	—	10
Saturday	15	—	—
Sunday	—	—	—
Total Minutes	25	15	10 = 50 min.

WEEK #2

	Swim	Bike	Run
Monday	10	—–	—–
Tuesday	—–	—–	—–
Wednesday	—–	—–	15
Thursday	—–	25	—–
Friday	—–	—–	—–
Saturday	15	—–	—–
Sunday	—–	—–	—–
Total Minutes	25	25	15 = 65 min.

WEEK #3

	Swim	Bike	Run
Monday	15	—–	—–
Tuesday	—–	15	—–
Wednesday	—–	—–	—–
Thursday	—–	—–	15
Friday	—–	20	—–
Saturday	15	—–	—–
Sunday	—–	—–	—–
Total Minutes	30	35	15 = 80 min.

WEEK #4

	Swim	Bike	Run
Monday	15	—–	—–
Tuesday	—–	20	—–
Wednesday	—–	—–	—–
Thursday	—–	—–	20
Friday	15	—–	—–
Saturday	—–	25	—–
Sunday	—–	—–	—–
Total Minutes	30	45	20 = 95 min.

4 Week Average = 72 minutes per week

WEEK #5

	Swim	Bike	Run
Monday	20	—–	—–
Tuesday	—–	30	—–
Wednesday	—–	—–	15
Thursday	15	—–	—–
Friday	—–	25	—–
Saturday	—–	—–	15
Sunday	—–	—–	—–
Total Minutes	35	55	30 = 120 min.

WEEK #6

	Swim	Bike	Run
Monday	20	—	—
Tuesday	—	35	—
Wednesday	—	—	20
Thursday	25	—	—
Friday	—	30	—
Saturday	—	—	20
Sunday	—	—	—
Total Minutes	45	65	40 = 150 min.

WEEK #7

	Swim	Bike	Run
Monday	25	—	—
Tuesday	—	35	—
Wednesday	—	—	25
Thursday	30	—	—
Friday	—	40	—
Saturday	—	—	25
Sunday	—	—	—
Total Minutes	55	75	50 = 180 min

WEEK #8

	Swim	Bike	Run
Monday	35	—	—
Tuesday	—	40	—
Wednesday	—	—	30
Thursday	30	—	—
Friday	—	45	—
Saturday	—	—	30
Sunday	—	—	—
Total Minutes	65	85	60 = 210 min.

Second 4 Week Average = 165 minutes per week

11

Racing

Racing or Not

Now that you have prepared as an athlete—you are training and getting fit—you might decide to enter a race. Many local running groups sponsor kids' events along with adult ones. Bike tours with organized groups are fun for kids. If you join a kids' swim group, they will have meets with other swim teams. Or you can enter an event like the Rainbo®/Colonial™ Bread Ironkids, which is a triathlon just for kids.

The Day Before

You are nervous.

It's the day before your first tri-kid race.

You have to get yourself ready, and the easiest way of doing it is to break the entire event into smaller parts.

The day before a race is "check day." Check all of your gear to make sure that it works, and fix anything that doesn't. You should already have everything you will need and have tried it in training first. You should have already done workouts that covered the length of the run one day, the bike another day, and the swim distance on another.

You need to look at the checklist of what you will need

to race. Check off what you are bringing, right here in the book, to make sure that you haven't forgotten anything.

Triathlon Race Equipment Checklist

Swim	Bike	Run
Racing suit	Helmet	Running shoes
Goggles	Bike	Visor/hat
Towel	Bike accessories	Running shorts
Gear bag	Sunglasses/eye	Food
Swim cap	protection	*Optional:*
	Shoes/cleats	Socks
	Race number	Sunscreen
	Water bottles	
	Optional:	
	Safety pins	
	Cycling shorts	
	Food	
	Water bucket to rinse feet	
	Socks	
	Cycling gloves	
	Fanny pack	
	Vaseline	

And how do you stop being nervous the day before? You probably can't, so just accept that everyone else feels about the same way.

The Day of The Race

Arrive an hour early and check in with the officials. The race organizers will mark your race number on your body with a felt pen. Then go to the transition area and set out all of your gear. Again, check all of your gear to make sure that everything is the way that you want it. Put down a towel next to your bike and put your running/cycling shoes on it. Put your helmet on your handlebars, and put the bike in the right gear for when you take off.

Stop. Look at everything. Is it all there?

Check the checklist. Did you set your gear out in the order in which you are going to use things?

Leave the transition area. Go to the swim area and look at how you exit the pool and how far it is to the transition area.

When you go to the races, you need to keep your equipment organized.

Next, go look at the run area—do you know the course? Look at the finish line and see where the banners are hung—crossing that line means that you are a winner.

When the announcer begins to call the age division waves, that is, those kids who will be in the same age and starting group as you, go to the pool. Spend at least five minutes stretching, and try to relax. There will be a lot of excitement and noise as announcements are made over the loud speaker, but don't get too distracted. Follow all the announced instructions exactly.

The Sound of the Starter's Signal

Usually the starter begins your wave with a countdown announced over a bullhorn. As you wait for that announcement, remember that you have trained for this day and that the most important part of it is to do your best and to have fun.

The starter yells, "Go!" and you are off. Swim under control, at a pace that you can hold through the entire distance. You should be tired at the end of the swim, but not *too* tired. Leave the pool area under control, and enter the transition. Try to be quick through the transition, as wasting time during this pit-stop is just that—wasted. Leave the transition area with both you and your bike under control.

During the bike race, keep in mind that not all of the other kids have as much experience as you. Give them plenty of room if you pass and shout to warn them if you are nearby. Ride under control. Do not go at a speed any faster than you can ride the entire race—that means that you ride as fast for the first mile as you do the last one.

At the end of the bike, enter the transition area, rack your bike, and prepare for the run. Again, don't waste time resting in the transition, but instead go quickly on to the run. Watch for other runners and cyclists in the transition area, as there will be a lot of activity there.

Using the even-pacing principle, run the entire race smoothly and at the same speed. Breathe deeply as you run, and ask yourself the question, "Am I having fun?" The answer had better be yes, or there is something wrong.

As you approach the finish banner, look up and check the clock. Remember what the time says, because this is a starting point for you. As you train and grow up, your times will improve, but this day should be one that stays in your memory for a long time to come. When you cross the line, you become a tri-kid!

After the Race

It's time to party!

Enjoy—you should feel great, because it is such an accomplishment to finish your first triathlon.

There is always food for the contestants, so eat and drink lots. You need to put both the calories and the fluids back into your body.

Put on your finisher's T shirt.

And, most of all, feel proud—we are proud of you.

Post-race parties are the time for laughter and celebration.

Imagine yourself on the winner's stand.

12

Winning

As the Rainbo®/Colonial™ Bread Ironkids say, "Every Finisher Is a Winner."

They're right.

There are other ways to measure winning that you should think about, because winning isn't just about being first. Winning is accomplishing your goals. You are a winner if you accomplish any one of these Seven Goals of a Winner.

The Seven Goals of a Winner

1. You did the best you could that day.
2. You made a new friend.
3. You had fun.
4. You finished strong.
5. You were responsible for yourself.
6. You tried your hardest.
7. You set a PR (personal record).

Many things make you a winner, not just your finishing place. If you set a PR (personal record), then write it down. That is now a lifetime best, and you should be proud of that. I know that if you practice the principles in *Triathlons for Kids,* you will have a lifetime of PRs.

Remember the story of the train engine that puffed its

I think I can, and I DID IT!

My Goal as a Winner: _____

I accomplished this Goal on: _____ , _____
                              (month)   (day)   (year)

Name: _____

School/Team/Event: _____

way to the top of a mountain saying, "I think I can! I think I can! I think I can!"? That's the way success in sports works, too—you have to think you can, and then you can. The path to success is not easy, but you can reach any goal you set, if you look at it as just a series of tiny steps toward an end.

Along the way there should be lots of rewards. One example is the "I Think I Can! And I Did It!" certificate. Fill one out and put it up each time you accomplish one of the Seven Goals of a Winner.

My next-door neighbor, Chrissie Cippa, visited me one day and became interested in a certain trophy that I had won. I told Chrissie, "You can take my trophy home, and when you win one of your own, you can give it back to me." One proud day, Chrissie knocked at my door with my trophy in one hand and the trophy she had just won at a swim meet in the other.

For Chrissie that day, winning meant returning my trophy to me with pride. For you, winning can mean all kinds of things, and what I want to see for you are the walls of your room and hallways of your home filled with "I Think I Can! And I Did It!" certificates, because I know that being a winner in sports means being a winner in life.

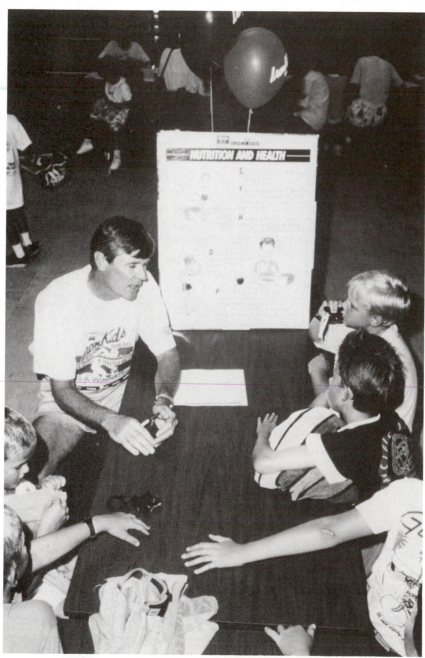

One part of the R/C Bread Ironkids program is to teach children good foods to eat and eating habits.

13

Eating

Several years ago, I appeared on the Oprah Winfrey Show. The show was on childhood obesity—why more kids today are fat than ever before. I was there because I had just written a book on the subject of weight loss titled *The Equilibrium Plan: Balancing Diet and Exercise for Lifetime Fitness*.

The three other guests were all kids who had fought the war against fat and lost. The next day, I watched a videotape of the show and was horrified. During the one-hour show, there were 18 commercials, all about food. Not only that, but all of the commercials advertised high-fat, high-sugar foods. There was only one commercial that showed a healthy food—strawberries. But at the end of the strawberry commercial, the advertisers put Cool Whip on top of the berries. It was an ad for an unhealthy food, Cool Whip, hidden behind a healthy one.

Some of my friends' kids play something called the "Prime-Time Kid" game whenever they watch TV. They take the disguises off the ads and expose the hidden messages in them. Here's how you can play, too. For example, a cereal that advertises "eight essential vitamins and minerals" *sounds* good for you, but the game is to be the first to ask, "How many of those vitamins and minerals are in the food, and what's just added in on top?" Or if the commercial says that a bread "builds bodies

12 ways," ask the advertiser what the 12 ways are. Or, for the chocolate cakes with pink marshmallow coating, you could ask, "If it isn't good to feed to my dog, why would I eat it?"

There is No Mystery

Nutritionists today agree that there is no mystery to a healthy diet and that there are no secret foods or supplements you need to eat. In fact, the only one way for you to eat right is pretty obvious, and that is by eating a variety of healthy, fresh foods.

The only real mystery in the nutrition game is how to win the war against vending machines, fast-food outlets, other kids' pressure, and television advertising.

The Rainbo®/Colonial™ Bread IronKids nutritional program is filled with great ideas that support their IronKids Triathlon program and is available for students and teachers. Call your local Rainbo Bakery and ask for the educational kit, "Reach for the Pride™."

A proper diet balances the four food groups. These food groups also balance the six basic nutrients: protein, fat, carbohydrates, water, vitamins, and minerals. Of these basic nutrients, the most important to a triathlete are the complex carbohydrates like potatoes, pasta, vegetables, wheat breads, and rice.

Learn To Cook

One of the best ways to learn to eat right is to learn to cook right. Children can start to learn to cook by the time they are four. You can bake nutrient-packed cookies using oatmeal, raisins, or peanut butter. Learn to make milk shakes with bananas and other fruit and nuts. There are lots of great foods that you can make that will fuel your engine with high-performance energy.

The most important meal that you can learn to prepare is breakfast. I'll repeat this, because it is that important: breakfast is *the* most important meal of the day. Yet kids skip breakfast more than any other meal. It just doesn't make any sense, especially if you want to be a good athlete and student.

So learn to make a real breakfast, not a "junk cereal" one. That means preparing fruit juice, toast, milk, *and* a healthy, not too sweet, cereal.

Overfat

The main reason that kids are overfat (wrongly called overweight) is not because of what they eat or from overeating. Kids today are overfat mostly because of what they don't do—they don't exercise or participate in enough calorie-burning activities or sports.

All kids have to choose between sports and sitting activities, such as watching television and playing computer games. Overfat kids can find success and not get picked on by sitting and watching video screens—it makes it very easy for them not to be active.

The real solution for overfat kids is movement. Overfat kids often have a tough time in team sports, but individual sports like swimming, cycling, and running or walking can be ideal for them. These sports are non-competitive and rewarding, and they are the highest calorie-burning activities of any major sports.

Some of you may, if you are overfat, think that you will "grow out of it as you get taller." Wrong. If overfat kids stay overfat as they grow, their bodies will just grow more fat cells which will stay with them all their lives. If you are an overfat kid, you will always be heavier than fit kids, unless you change into *being* a fit kid.

Drugs

There is no need for them—in sports or in your life. They destroy the lives of professional athletes, and they will do the same to you.

Calories

Kids eat smaller amounts of food and fewer calories than adults, so the calories you eat need to be densely packed with nutrients for your body to use. There is less room for "empty calories" in the foods you eat, because you eat fewer calories overall.

When you work out, you burn calories. The "Burning Calories Worksheet" is a way for you to find out about the principles of burning calories through training. Read the worksheet now and fill in the answers.

Triathlons for Kids
BURNING CALORIES WORKSHEET

Data:
- Running burns about 100 calories per mile.
- Bicycling consumes about 40 calories per mile.
- Swimming burns about 24 calories per 100 yards.
- Running consumes about 10 calories per minute.
- Swimming uses about 12 calories per minute.
- Bicycling burns about 9 calories per minute.

Questions:

Write the answer after each queston:

1. Which activity burns the most calories in 30 minutes?
   Answer:_____

2. Which activity burns the least number of calories in 10 minutes?
   Answer:_____

3. If you swam for 30 minutes, how many calories would you burn?
   Answer:_____

4. If you ran for 15 minutes, how many calories would you burn?
   Answer:_____

5. If you bicycled for 45 minutes, how many calories would you burn?
   Answer:_____

6. How many calories would everyone burn all together, if four of you ran for 30 minutes?
   Answer:_____

7. If you swam for five minutes, biked for 10 minutes, and ran for 15 minutes how many calories would you burn?
   Answer:_____

8. How many calories do you burn if you compete in the Rainbo®/Colonial™ Bread Ironkids Triathlon* if you are a junior? If you are a senior?

Answer:_____ Junior

_____Senior

9. What is the difference in calories burned in one hour, between running and cycling?

Answer:_____

10. What is the difference in calories burned in minutes, between swimming and running?

Answer:_____

* The distances are as follows:

Junior: 100-yard swim, 6.2-mile bike, .6-mile run.

Seniors: 200-yard swim, 12.4-mile bike, 1.2-mile run.

ANSWERS

1. Swimming burns the most calories.
2. Bicycling consumes the least number of calories.
3. 360 calories would be burned.
4. You would burn 150 calories in 15 minutes.
5. You would burn 405 calories.
6. Four of you would each burn 300 calories, or 1,200 calories altogether.
7. You would burn 60 calories swimming, 90 calories bicycling, 150 calories running. Altogether you would burn 300 calories.
8. If you were a junior, you would burn 332 calories, and if you were a senior, 664.
9. The difference is 60 calories.
10. Two calories.

World champion triathlete Erin Baker eats 4,000 to 6,000 calories per day. That's because she trains two to five hours every day in her three sports. The number of calories that you eat depends on how active you are (or how un-active).

The basic fitness idea to know is that "calories in must equal calories out," if you want to stay slim and strong, not over-fat. If you eat more (calories "in") than you burn through movement (calories "out"), you will gain fat. Your job is to balance your food groups and the calories you eat. When you have done this, you have passed your first basic course in nutrition.

14

Staying Healthy

The three sports of triathlon—swimming, cycling, and running—are considered "safe sports." This means that they are low in injuries and risks because they are not contact sports like football or soccer. However, even in safe sports, injuries occur. Yet most of them can be prevented if you, the triathlete, know what to do.

Hopefully, most of you are hooked on sports for life. I am, and I know that at some time in my athletic career I will be (and have been) injured. It hasn't happened often, because I listen to my body and pay attention to it when I feel pain or soreness. A lot of kids don't pay enough attention to their bodies and get hurt because of it.

The U.S. Consumer Product Safety Commission reports that 4 million children were brought in for emergency room treatment for sports injuries last year. Add to this another 8 million kids who were treated for injuries by family physicians, and that's a lot of kids getting hurt.

Most of these severe injuries could be prevented if the problem was caught early and treated properly. That means that you can't pretend that you don't hurt—the fear of missing practice or looking like a wimp isn't worth the price you pay by not getting help.

Let's look at a few of the most common injuries that kids get.

Injuries can lead to frustration.

Overuse Injuries

You are growing at this stage in your life. This means that your bones are soft and your ligaments, tendons, and muscles are tight. The good side to being in a growing stage is that your body heals itself much faster than an adult body.

Overuse injuries happen when you train harder than your growing body is ready to—too much, too soon. Examples of overuse include shin splints, sore Achilles' tendons, swimmer's shoulder, and over-training fatigue.

Overuse injuries happen slowly and can sneak up on you, not like broken bones or sprains, which happen all of a sudden so you know that there is something wrong. The damage to a growing kid's soft and hard tissues, caused by an overuse injury that is not treated or is not detected, can lead to permanent damage, so being careful in the first place is the best way to go!

Patellar Pain Syndrome

This is the number one injury that pediatric sports medicine clinics treat. It is also known as Osgood-Schlatter discase, but it is actually an overuse injury, not a disease. It is recognized by pain, swelling and tenderness in the area around the kneecap. It usually afflicts girls between 8 and 13 years-old and boys between 10 and 15. A medical check-up and rest are required.

Imbalance Injuries

These are injuries caused by a lack of balanced muscle groups, which are in turn caused by poor posture, overdeveloped muscle groups, or anatomical weaknesses. For example, runners develop their hamstrings (back of the upper leg) more than any other muscle. Cyclists develop their quadriceps (the front upper leg muscle). If you don't develop both, you can cause an imbalance that can result in muscle injuries.

Back pain is most often caused by imbalances, especially of the back muscles, but also from weak stomach muscles, and a lack of flexibility.

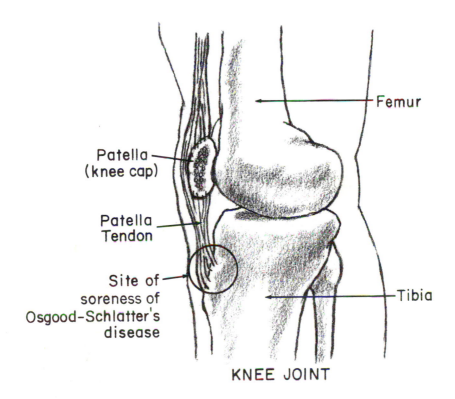

KNEE JOINT

Strengthening exercises and cross-training can heal muscle imbalances, but you should always be careful to avoid training on any area that is hurt and not yet healed.

Growth Plate Injuries

The growth plate is the part of the bone where the bone grows. When you are fully grown, the growth plate unites with the bone and disappears. Damaging this area can result in a disruption of your growth.

On one hand, sports activities stimulate the bones to become stronger and tougher. Research has shown that athletic kids have bones that are larger and healthier than those of non-athletic kids. But if you over-stress your bones, they can become inflamed and hamper your growth.

There are three types of injuries to the growth plate: a break, a crushing injury, and a separation of the growth plate. If you fall while running or cycling, you can crush or break a bone. Repeated pounding from heavy-footed running on hard surfaces can cause separation of the growth plate.

Growth plate injuries are not too common, making up only six percent of all injuries in kids' athletics.

Common Discomforts

Side aches. Side aches or stitches don't last forever, but they sure can put a stop to a fun training session. Generally, they seem to be caused by over-exertion or not being in good enough shape yet. The exact cause of side aches is unknown, but they might also be from gas that is caught in the upper intestines. Here are a couple of tricks you can try in order to stop the pain:

- Put pressure from your fingers directly on the place that hurts.
- Massage the area with your whole hand.
- Straighten your back and stretch tall.
- Relax your breathing and slow down the number of breaths you are taking per minute.
- Lean forward, bending at the waist.

Post-workout nausea. Some of you may feel like throwing-up after a hard workout. It can be caused by eating too much just before a workout, or by not eating enough, so that your body doesn't have enough calories to work with. It can also be caused by dehydration (not drinking enough fluids). Change your drinking and eating patterns and see what helps.

Blisters. They can be caused by shoes that don't fit well, that have tight spots, or are wet. Small blisters can be covered with medicated cream and a bandage. Large blisters should be drained with a sterilized needle (*by an adult*), then treated with medicated cream and a covering. Pay attention to them—they can get infected.

Muscle cramps. What feels like knotted muscles are involuntary contractions of the muscle. It is not known what causes them—it could be a lack of sodium, potassium, calcium, or a vitamin complex. To help get rid of the pain, stretch the joint, massage the area, and "walk it off" by gently moving the muscle. Then, look at your diet, and if cramps happen frequently, change your drinking and eating habits and see if that helps.

Prevention of Injuries

The best way to prevent sports injuries is to use the team approach. The players on your team are your training partners, parents, coaches, physical education teachers, medical supervisors, and the most important player of all—you. If you have your team working with you and you are taking responsibility for your actions, you can cut down the number of injuries and the amount of "downtime" you will have.

If you add modern training techniques and good equipment to your team, you have the best odds of not being hurt, or of being hurt only rarely. Here are some other prevention tips:

- Work up to high-intensity workouts slowly.
- Don't make big changes all at once, instead make small, gradual ones.
- Don't increase your workout distance by more than 10 to 20 percent each week.
- Don't stress yourself when breaking in new equipment.
- Warm up correctly.
- Check your diet—is it good enough for a triathlete? (See Chapter 13.)
- *Listen* to your body, and do as it asks.
- Train often in small amounts, not lots off and on.

Treatment

Getting treatment right away is the only smart move for any injury. For overuse injuries, the most common treatment is RICE. RICE stands for <u>r</u>est, <u>i</u>ce, <u>c</u>ompression, and <u>e</u>levation, and rest is the most important of the four treatments.

<u>Rest:</u> This means complete rest. No workouts until the pain has totally gone away.

<u>Ice:</u> Ice the entire area several times each day. Ice will make the swelling go down and increase the blood flow to the area. Use an ice bag or even a bag of frozen vegetables and massage the area. Get the injured area very cold for 10 minutes, then take the ice off for 20 minutes, and then put the ice back on for another 10 minutes.

<u>Compression:</u> If there is swelling, quickly wrap the area firmly, but not so tightly as to cut off the blood flow. Compression is used to keep too much fluid from coming into the area, so that healing can begin.

<u>Elevation:</u> Keep the injured area higher than your head or, if it is a lower body injury, up off the floor. This also keeps the area from getting too much blood and becoming swollen.

Most kids' doctors agree that for minor injuries to muscles and joints, you should "wait and see" just how badly you are hurt before going to a hospital or doctor's office. Still, as an athlete, you are responsible to "listen" to your body. So, if the pain from the injury is too much, let an adult know, so that they can get you to a doctor quickly.

Believe it or not, you can also benefit from an injury—it is a way to learn something. Remember and think about what went wrong, and you may not have to ever make that same mistake again.

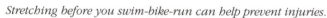

Stretching before you swim-bike-run can help prevent injuries.

15

You, the Parent

When I was a child, I thought as a child and played as a child. When I grew up, I gave up childish things, became a triathlete and discovered that I was a child again. That "child's" play is just what the sport of triathlon means to many adults—it's a chance to return to our playful youth where we swam for fun, biked for transportation, and ran on school playgrounds.

As an adult and as a parent, you have the chance to play with your child and enjoy sharing the positive sports experiences that lead them to feeling good about themselves, fitness, and you.

We ask that kids set goals and then work towards accomplishing them. But as a parent, have you set goals for your involvement with your children? For their athletic participation? Here are some of the goals that you might consider making a part of your game plan:

Goals for Parents of Athletes

- To support my child regardless of their athletic talent.
- To be realistic about my child's athletic abilities.
- To prohibit my child from participating in a program that places unreasonable demands upon them,

demands that could cause physical or emotional scars.

- To participate only in programs that benefit my child.
- To help in the development of the physical, emotional, and psychological components of my young athlete.
- To learn and teach that there are more important things to gain from sports than being number one.
- To provide a safe and healthy sports environment that includes the proper equipment and training methods.
- To help my child be committed to the joy of sports as well as to maximize her or his full athletic potential.
- To teach my child how to play safely.
- To allow and encourage my child's creative physical expression. Kids will not always be able to stick exactly to a regimen; accept this and encourage and love them anyway.
- To lead my child into a lifetime of physical activity.
- To teach my child to set realistic goals.
- Not to relive my athletic past through my child's present.
- To control my emotions at events.
- To be a cheerleader for *all* the children involved in an event.

- To respect my child's coaches and teachers and communicate openly with them.
- To lead a healthy lifestyle myself and be a positive role model.
- To make sure that my child knows that I love them and am proud of their performance, win or lose.

Because of the modern structure of our sports organizations, programs today are highly structured and adult-controlled and can encourage physical and psychological abuse. We cannot tolerate sports programs that teach counter-

Supporting your child through the finish line and into your arms is one of the definitions of love.

productive values to our youth, nor can we accept a sedentary lifestyle perpetuated by television and computer games.

Triathletic participation offers an alternative to both.

Listening to your children as well as training with them counts.

The Parent as Athletic Role Model

Children naturally model themselves after adults. You are the best example of an athletic lifestyle that your child has. If you are active, if you eat a balanced and calorie-controlled diet, if you are excited about participating in fitness activities, your child will probably follow.

This is a call for you to live the lifestyle which you want for your children. As you feel the benefits of fitness, so will your tri-kid. If you temper your program with patience and increase your knowledge of exercise and its relationship to emotional and physical development, your child will prosper. Start by reading this book together—discuss the information and learn together.

If you commit to the long-term—a lifetime fitness lifestyle—you are providing a head start to those you raise.

The Downside

Sports are not necessarily beneficial to all children. Dr. Bruce Ogilvie, a leading sports sociologist, states that sports participation can sometimes be harmful and psychologically traumatic. As a parent, you can't allow your children to participate in programs that place unreasonable demands on them—you can't allow the emotional and physical damage that can lead to permanent scars.

You have a responsibility to set healthy goals for yourself and not to set your children's goals, but to aid them in wisely developing their own. Your goals must encourage a healthy, positive atmosphere for physical activity and sports.

Parents' goals may not coincide with children's. If this happens, it can lead to open conflict between you both. Don't allow adult egos to turn sports into a training ground for future stars, since that just reduces the children to pawns in a game that they didn't choose.

Remember, too, that the amount of time you'll need to invest in your child's athletic development will vary with how physically skilled they are. The child that has a tough time balancing on a bike or learning the freestyle needs more help in developing their skills than the superstar.

A lifetime of physical activity for your child counts more than their being a sports hero for a few years, so encourage sports activities for their intrinsic value. There are plenty of lasting rewards if you do.

The Family

You know about the family that plays together—they tend to stay together. This is partly because the best potential atmosphere for a positive sports experience is within the supportive family unit. Going on sports vacations together is a great idea. A camping vacation can teach the rigors of hiking and provide an appreciation for the outdoors. Participating in a family sports camp can also be very rewarding.

Parental support is the key. Most coaches and teachers agree that they prefer a meddling parent to one who doesn't care. The former can be trained, the latter has to be motivated. Still, while a child must get support from the home to be successful in sports, it must be understood that support is different from pushing. Overbearing parents may be well-intentioned, but their behavior does not lead to a positive sports experience.

If you are a parent who wants a prediction of your child athlete's potential because you are wondering about college scholarships, Olympic medals, and breakfast cereal endorsements, then read this section again because you have missed the entire point. Your responsibility is to lay the foundation of a positive experience, not to reach for monetary gain or parental ego-development.

If you are a parent who wants to know now whether your child has a chance to become a professional athlete, because you don't want to waste your time on sports if they can't, then you will never be able to lay the groundwork to that or any other firm foundation.

Little League Syndrome

Approximately 80 percent of children drop out of competitive sports by the age of 12. One of the causes of this appalling statistic is the Little League Syndrome, where parents, coaches, and sometimes even the young athlete choose achievement over fun—at all costs. Fortunately, the "Little League" parents and insensitive, win-oriented coaches are a minority; most parents and coaches have good intentions. Still, sometimes the syndrome takes hold unconsciously, and children are made to act like miniature versions of stressed-out adults.

There are three different symptoms which children who've been touched by the Little League Syndrome display.

The first is the "Wash-Out Symptom." Those who washout leave sports because they are discouraged. In team sports, they sit on the bench or don't make the team. In triathlons, they lose interest because it is too hard or boring. In truth, children wash-out when sports are no longer fun.

The second is the "Burn-out Symptom." Children quit participating because they've had too much of everything—training, success, pressure—at too early an age. It is a combination of psychological fatigue, physical staleness, and anxiety, which results in a lack of energy and enthusiasm for sports. Burn-out is common among swimmers because of the double-workouts and tedious hours.

The third is the "Superstar Symptom." You can see this in children who are overly competitive, compulsive, and dominant. They seek approval and need reassurance. Though the superstar rarely quits, the damage is severe, since they are maladjusted and overindulged to the point of psychological injury.

As "Digger" Phelps, the University of Notre Dame's basketball coach explains, "Worse than the physical risk in playing sports today is the possibility of creating a monster, a primadonna, a kid who thinks (s)he's a superstar, who believes the world revolves around her/him and around sports."

The center of sports programs needs to be the child, and if their primary purpose is participation, then feed their need to have fun. Supporting their quest for fun is more important than nurturing them with achievement and its flipside, failure.

16

Teachers and Coaches

The importance of your child athlete's teachers and coaches cannot be overemphasized, and you should do your best to ensure that your child's other role models and guardians are good ones. However, there is no need for paranoia when choosing a physical education program for your child—just stay involved and observant and all should go well.

Coaches

As a parent, you need to do your homework. You need to have your children in a swim/bike/run program that allows them the most opportunity for success. One of the best ways to assure this is to talk to the coach and ask him or her (as well as parents of kids already in the program) questions such as:

- How many children are in the program?
- Does the coach emphasize participation or winning?
- What type of certification is required for the coach?
- What is the coach's philosophy?
- Are only talented athletes given attention, or are all children, regardless of ability, encouraged to participate?
- What other sports has the coach taught?

As a parent, spend the time to meet your children's coaches and observe their program.

- What is the coach's athletic background?
- Who are some of the other kids in the program?
- What do the other kids and parents have to say about the coach?
- What options do you have if you don't like the coach?
- How frequently are the coach's athletes injured?
- What are the wash-out and burn-out rates of the coach's athletes?

Next, you need to match your child's goals with those of the coach. Does your child want to socialize more than focus on developing skill and physical conditioning? That's OK, and it's important to know if they do, because figuring out your child's prime motivations is the key of making a good match between program and child.

One way to screen coaching talent is to find out if the coach is certified. Even though coaching certification is not yet required, it should be mandatory. It is your responsibility to enroll your kids in organized sports programs with a certified coach at the helm, or urge an uncertified coach to pursue this goal.

When coaching certification becomes mandatory, it will be a win-win-win situation. Coaches will win: they'll be trained and knowledgeable in injury prevention and the principles of fitness. Parents will win: their children will be in programs being lead by qualified instructors. The kids will win: they'll be better trained, with better skills and fewer injuries.

As a coach, I know how difficult the job really is. Sometimes it seems that everyone is angry at you. At other times, coaching is the most rewarding job that I have ever had. If you can set up the win-win-win game, the grandstands will cheer, the athletes will always know that you made a difference in their lives, and the parents will give you the respect that you have earned.

Teachers

The job of the classroom teacher and the coach are quite different. Coaches are under the microscope—if they win or lose they are analyzed in the newspaper, discussed in the grandstands, and publicly scrutinized.

Teachers, especially in physical education, are, in comparison, relatively obscure. If they fail, few know it—there are no scoreboards or finish-line clocks.

There are a number of useful tools available to teachers today to develop successful curriculum programs for the young triathlete. The Long Beach, California, Miller Children's Hospital has prepared a booklet titled "Miller Children's Mini-Marathon Training Program." The booklet includes integrated classroom activities, certificates, logs, suggested reading for educators, and a detailed running program for children.

Rainbo®/Colonial™ Bread, the sponsor of Ironkids, also has extensive materials available for teachers. Contact them through your local Rainbo®/Colonial™ Bakery or through Traksports, St. Louis, Missouri (or phone 314-241-8100). The Rainbo®/Colonial™ Bread Ironkids program is one of the best I know that is sponsored by a company, not an educational institute. Both of these programs integrate conditioning with classroom activities that include math, vocabulary, nutrition, goal-setting, and others.

In addition, AAHPERD, the American Association of Health, Physical Education, Recreation, and Dance, in Reston, Virginia, has a new program titled "Physical Best," which is a comprehensive physical fitness education and assessment program designed for teachers. Physical Best is the first program to combine assessment of health-related fitness with practical classroom instructional materials that teach kids how and why to stay fit for a lifetime.

As a credentialed teacher, I recognize the importance of integrating physical education with the other aspects of a child's education. Hopefully, this book, *Triathlons for Kids,* can provide you with foundation material that you can use both inside and outside of your classroom. The first section of the book was written for children to read. Encourage them to do so. Take the material and use it in your curriculum design. The charts, graphs, and equations provide you with math material, and Chapter 3, "Let's Talk," can be built into a language module, since it includes spelling, vocabulary, and definitions.

As a teacher, you know that most children want the same thing—to play and have fun in a positive sports experience.

Let's provide that for them.

17

Your Child, the Triathlete

Self-Esteem

The Rainbo®/Colonial™ Bread Ironkids program focuses on building children's self-esteem. Sure, they also want to sell bread products—that's their business. But the company's contributions to our youth really have been exemplary. They are committed to providing children with an opportunity to say at the finish line, "I am an Ironkid." Those are powerful words. To your children, it means that they are strong, fit, athletic, successful, and worthy of respect.

As a parent, imagine the effect on your youngsters' growth, year after year, as they get to the finish line and say, "I am an Ironkid." Imagine what this will mean as they grow into adults. By your support and encouragement, you will give them one of the most valuable gifts a parent can offer beyond love: self-esteem.

You have set the stage for a lifetime of physical health and well-being.

You have created a family atmosphere where sports participation is the accepted lifestyle.

You are the winner, a winning parent with a winning child.

Winning

In combative sports, winning is defined as defeating the opponent, conquering them.

In the triathletic way, winning is what happens when a person participates to their potential. This is the perspective that sports should communicate to our children, that winning is doing your best. Sports can teach personal, as well as athletic, excellence.

Last Christmas day, I volunteered to help a couple of friends, Gene and Cathy Meyers. Gene is a special education teacher at a local boys ranch, and that Christmas there were six teenage boys there who didn't have a place to go home.

On that day, I suggested that we take six sports, play each for an hour, and then have dinner together. Each of us had our own agenda. Gene wanted to make sure everyone had fun. Cathy wanted to ensure fairness, so she became our official. I was in training for four Ironmans in the coming year, so I didn't want to get hurt. With these bounds set, before we started the first hour of flag football, I asked the boys what rules they wanted.

It was incredibly enlightening to me that the most important rule to them was one that I had never considered. Tom, a big 16-year-old who had been physically abused as an adolescent, said, "I want a rule that you can't make fun and laugh at anybody if they make a mistake, like drop the ball or fall."

All Tom wanted was to make sure that no one could get put down for goofing up (for being human). His rule was marvelously simple and fair, and it made me wonder why it isn't enforced in all of our activities—in business, relationships, *and* sports. It was especially appropriate to be reminded of that on Christmas day, because it is the spirit of love and respect that leads to a truly winning philosophy.

Competition

The winners, in our society as a whole, are the fiercest competitors. So why is it that I suggest that, for children's sports, competition should be de-emphasized and placing in first given a low priority?

I believe in the de-emphasis of competition for the sake of "winning," because cut-throat competitiveness generally results in children not learning or achieving the healthier values which sports can teach. During their early years, children need

Winning takes many forms.

to learn motor skills and develop their fitness. Competition viewed from the *winner/loser* perspective cuts off the learning process prematurely. Children are not physically, mentally, or emotionally prepared for the pressures of high-level competition.

Competition itself is not the culprit—it can be both healthy and not, competition is a medium. If the purpose of the competition is to participate to one's fullest, then it is healthy. If the purpose of the competition is to determine winners and losers, then it is probably less healthy.

Programs that emphasize positive sports experiences lead to kids' progressive improvement in skills and fitness, building firm foundations for future participation, not celebrity superstars.

Your children's only competition should be with themselves. A child who learns first to compete against their own clock or their own score will become a more confident, skillful teenager and adult.

Triathlons for kids should be fun. (Triathlons for adults should be, too!)

A Bill of Rights for Young Triathletes

Children need protection from the downside of sports—from coaches, parents, teachers, and even themselves. Here are 10 principles that are designed for the protection of the young triathlete and that should guide you in your decisions about their future and your place in it.

THE BILL OF RIGHTS FOR YOUNG TRIATHLETES

We believe that all young triathletes possess the following inalienable rights:

1. The right to have fun.
2. The right to get fit.
3. The right to be in charge.
4. The right to train at a level that equals their ability.
5. The right to say "no."
6. The right to be treated with respect and dignity.
7. The right to play as a child (not as an adult).
8. The right to a safe environment and safe equipment.
9. The right to information, coaches, and experiences.
10. The right to equal opportunity.

18

The Differences between Tri-Kids: Girls and Boys

There are many physical performance differences between boys and girls which researchers have busied themselves with measuring. But even today, little is known about the differences between the genders in such areas as motivation, attitude, or their reasons for participating athletically.

Physical Performance Differences

Thanks to the national concern about the physical fitness level of our youth, extensive tests have been conducted over many years to measure children's cardiovascular endurance, strength and muscular endurance, flexibility, and body composition (fatness). As a result of this research, "norms" have been established with which you can compare your tri-kids' scores (but *not* with which to judge them).

For triathletic success, the most important physical component is cardiorespiratory fitness, the ability of the large muscles to perform moderate- to high-intensity physical activity over extended periods of time. Indeed, cardiorespiratory conditioning is considered the most important aspect of any exercise program, because of the overall health benefits that it provides.

Although fitness tests for children in swimming and cycling do not exist, running tests for children have been com-

Norms in Minutes and Seconds for 1-Mile Run for Ages 5 through 14 Years

PERCENTILE	5	6	7	8	9	10	11	12	13	14
MALES										
95	9:02	9:06	8:06	7:58	7:17	6:56	6:50	6:27	6:11	5:51
75	11:32	10:55	9:37	9:14	8:36	8:10	8:00	7:24	6:52	6:36
50	13:46	12:29	11:25	11:00	9:56	9:19	9:06	8:20	7:27	7:10
25	16:05	15:10	14:02	13:29	12:00	11:05	11:31	10:00	8:35	8:02
5	18:25	17:38	17:17	16:19	15:44	14:28	15:25	13:41	10:23	10:32
FEMALES										
95	9:45	9:18	8:48	8:45	8:24	7:59	7:46	7:26	7:10	7:18
75	13:09	11:24	10:55	10:35	9:58	9:30	9:12	8:36	8:18	8:13
50	15:08	13:48	12:30	12:00	11:12	11:06	10:27	9:47	9:27	9:35
25	17:59	15:27	14:30	14:16	13:18	12:54	12:10	11:35	10:56	11:43
5	19:00	18:50	17:44	16:58	16:42	17:00	16:56	14:46	14:55	16:59

(Age)

Adapted from health related physical fitness test manual, Reston, Virginia AAHPERD, 1980, and R. R. Pate, Norms for college students Reston, Virginia. AAHPERD, 1985

There are physical as well as emotional differences between girls and boys—learn them.

pleted, and norms have been set for the one-mile run for ages 5 through 14 years. (See chart on page 106.)

It is important to notice the differences between the boys' and girls' scores. The 6-year-old boys who rank in the 75th percentile are 14 percent faster than girls the same age, and, by the age of 14, boys become 25 percent faster than girls. It is a damaging myth that girls and boys can compete equally with one another in endurance activities until they reach puberty. Actually, their processes of physical development are substantially different from very early on.

If you want, you can use this normative information to test your children and see in which percentile they rank. The point is not to compare your children with others, but to give you a reference point for their improvement. With triathletic training, your child's cardiorespiratory fitness level will improve dramatically—it is one of the sure rewards of any conditioning program.

Differences in Preferences

Girls and boys enjoy basically the same sports, and the great news is that the triathletic sports of swimming, cycling, and running are ranked by both sexes as three of the top five. Both boys and girls acknowledge that swimming and running (racing/sprinting) are the sports that they play most frequently for fun, with the third place activities being cycling for girls and baseball for boys.

Popularity of Sports

GIRLS			BOYS		
	Rank	% Who Participate		Rank	% Who Participate
Swimming	1	39%	Swimming	1	36%
Running	2	32%	Running	2	33%
Bicycling	3	15%	Baseball	3	23%
Playing on a Playground	4	14%	Soccer	4	21%
			Bicycling	5	15%
Gymnastics	5	10%	Playing on a Playground	6	11%
Walking	5	10%			
Basketball	7	8%	Football	7	10%
Climbing	8	8%	Basketball	8	9%
Hiking	9	8%	Climbing	9	8%
Playing (unspecified)	10	8%	Hiking	10	7%
Soccer	11	6%	Walking	11	7%
Ballet/Dance	12	5%	T Ball	12	5%

From AAHPERD (The American Alliance of Health, Physical Education, Recreation, and Dance) for ages 6-10 years

The most significant gender difference lies not in sports preferences, but in the frequency of participation. An average of 15.4 percent of boys participate in any one of the boys' top 12 sports, compared with only 13.6 percent of the girls who participate in any one of their top 12.

Parents

Frequency of participation is equally an issue for these same children's parents, since approximately 50 percent of parents say they never participate in vigorous exercise—never. This can be interpreted by children of both sexes to mean that their parents don't value exercise.

Of the parents who do exercise, both mothers and fathers do so with their children less than one day per week on the average. Within this limited time frame, mothers exercise with equal frequency with both their daughters and their sons. Fathers, though, discriminate against their daughters and prefer to exercise primarily with their male children. Fathers exercise 50 days per year with their sons on the average, versus only 35 days per year with their daughters. This disparity increases with the children's age—as boys become more involved in team sports, so do their fathers, to the detriment of the female children.

Whatever the genders involved, the underlying problem remains the critical lack of time parents spend exercising with their children. Starting a triathletic regimen is one way to create both the opportunity and the responsibility for many hours, days, weeks, and months of shared parent-child athletic interaction.

19

Answers to Important Questions

Question: How old should a child be before beginning competition?

Answer: It depends on the sport *and* the child. Some gymnasts start competing at the age of 4, but that sport is rather an exception. Generally, if the competitive programs stress skill development, participation by all children, and fun, then competitions can begin as early as 6. Remember, though, that most sports specialists believe that a child gains no advantage over other children by starting competitions before the age of 8, and some sports, like baseball and tennis, require complex ball-handling skills which even most 8 year-olds do not yet possess. Tri-kid competitions are designed for fun and to build your child's self-esteem and, for these reasons, are healthy at quite a young age.

Question: When you mix children and sports, someone always gets hurt. Is it worth it?

Answer: Fortunately for triathletes, most athletic injuries occur in the sports of football (20 percent), basketball (17 percent), roller skating (13 percent), and baseball (9 percent), not in swimming, cycling, or running. Overall, the long-term physical

Guidelines for Youth Developments

AGE (yrs)	7	8	9	10	11	12	13	14
	PLAY – fun and games (enjoyment more important than competition)							
		Technique Training – stroke, pedal, stride technique						
	Flexibility Training							
	Endurance starts with Aerobic Training							
							Anaerobic Training	
					Aerobic Intervals – short and easy			
							Serious Competition	
					Longer Workouts – build base			
	Develop Skills		Develop Base		Develop Skills and Base		Develop Speed and Competition	

(Left vertical axis label: Developmental Stages for Skills and Other Components to Swim, Bike, Run)

benefits of sports conditioning, such as stronger muscles and bones, not only outweigh the risk of injury, they *lessen* the risk. It is true that some injuries are an inevitable byproduct of sports, but most are preventable if:

- Children are trained for the symptoms and take responsibility for treatment of the symptom or subsequent injury.
- Coaches include warm-up and cool-down exercises in practice sessions.
- Children have the proper equipment to train safely.
- Everyone on the team—coaches, parents, athletes— stresses proper physical conditioning as a *year-round* activity, emphasizing both strength- and endurance-building programs, even in the off-season.
- If an injured child's need for full recovery, *before* reentering a sports activity, is taken seriously.
- Children are properly supervised and their physical state frequently assessed.
- Children are taught to follow the correct exercise forms: proper swim strokes, running style, and bicycling techniques. Using correct biomechanical forms reduces muscular and skeletal stress and lessens the chance of injury.

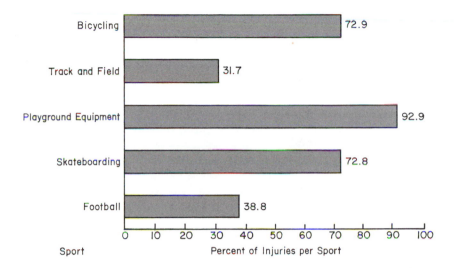

Bicycling — 72.9
Track and Field — 31.7
Playground Equipment — 92.9
Skateboarding — 72.8
Football — 38.8

Sport — Percent of Injuries per Sport

Question: I have heard that sports can be physically harmful to my daughter. Is this true?

Answer: It's difficult to imagine that we are into the decade of the 1990s, yet myths about the harmful physical effects of sports participation for girls and women still persist. The following are all *facts* about sports participation for females:

- The activities of swimming, cycling, and running do not damage the reproductive organs of girls or women. Care should always be taken to wear proper breast support, though, as breast tissue can become sore if stressed.

- Girls do not have a more fragile bone structure than boys and are not more likely to be injured.

- Intense sports competitions do not cause any permanent or long-term menstrual problems. Missed periods occasionally do occur, but generally only in *extremely* physically active or slender women.

- Strenuous participation in sports does not lead to problems in childbearing.

- Sports training for girls or women does not lead to the development of huge, bulging muscles.

Question: I want to encourage my child to try triathlon. How do I begin?

Answer: You start with yourself. If your child needs motivation and direction, there is no better place to start than with you, as role model. Both of you should sign up for a class at a local club or for a district recreation program and set up a weekly training schedule so that you work out several times a week together. Share this book, *Triathlons for Kids*—it was written for both of you to read and use. Also, reducing the number of hours that watching television is allowed never hurts. Work toward the day that your child crosses the finish line and proudly says, "I am a tri-kid," and you respond, "Yes, and I am a triathlete."

Question: My child spends some time every afternoon in front of the TV. Is this really a problem, and, if so, what should I do about it?

Answer: Recent research has pointed to a new pediatric disease—TV addiction. Spread over the course of a year, children spend as much time watching TV as they do in school.

Age	Hours of TV/Week
2-5 years	25 $\frac{1}{2}$ hours
6-11 years	23 hours

Every one-hour increase in television viewing per week results in a two percent increase in the prevalence of obesity. Children's inactive viewing hours are time stolen that could be spent in physical activity. As obesity is a major health threat, you must take it upon yourself to limit the amount of time your children are allowed to watch TV. Most studies recommend allowing children to view only one to two hours of TV each week. If your children complain of boredom, it is an opportunity to teach them to rely on themselves for ideas and for you to suggest active paths on which to build new habits and positive addictions.

Question: It worries me to have my children out of sight riding their bikes or running. What can I do?

Triathletic children train for many of the same reasons as their parents.

Answer: There are always fears anytime your child leaves your side—when they go to school, play at a neighbor's, stay after school, or come home afterwards. The best thing that you can do is to provide them with basic training in self-protection and safety. You should also provide them with the necessary safety equipment—helmets for when they bike, reflective gear if they're out at night, the right shoes and swim goggles that won't leak. Lastly, you must set rules and make sure they are understood—they must let you know who they are with, where they are going, and when they will return.

Question: What effect will a strenuous sports program have on my child's growth?

Answer: All, and I mean *all*, of the research points to the fact that physical activity leads to stronger bones, better muscle development, less obesity and fewer physical problems from over-fatness.

Question: My child won't join me in competitions—she says that it scares her. What can I do?

Answer: Talk with her and find out just what it is that scares her. Is she intimidated or afraid of failure? Or is she afraid of crowds and spectators, or does she worry that competing might be painful? Next, develop a strategy. Ask her to watch as a spectator, so that she knows what the event looks like. Then, ask if she would like to practice exactly the same event when no one else is around. Later, see if a couple of her friends can join her, so that the practice begins to resemble the event. With enough positive encouragement, good role-modeling from you and others, listening and teaching, and, of course, time, she will probably want to jump in and be a participant. Remember to always highlight the fun and play down the competitive side of the activity.

The most important action you can take is to be supportive: encourage, understand, and praise her. Lastly, note that according to sociologist Jay Coakley, "Since females are more likely than males to have learned that they are not expected to excel in particular tasks, especially those demanding experience in sports, they will be less motivated by competition involving physical skills," and try to reeducate your daughter accordingly.

20

The Sweet Spot in Sports—Kids

Athletes, musicians, and computer programmers all arrive at the sweet spot in life through the rhythm of their specialty. That rhythm is more than timing—it is a progressively intimate linking of thought and action that comes together in something beyond the person, the activity, and the moment.

As a long distance runner, I know that the most memorable runs are those when no matter how difficult it is physically, no matter how fast the pace or the pulse rate, the feeling is of effortlessness. The sweet spot occurs when my body's many parts link together and flow rhythmically, and my mind is in a similarly fluid, clear, and easy state—and knows it. It is that fulfilling moment that happens when mind and body come together.

As another example, drummers focus on timing and on syncopation. Every strike of the drummer's stick lasts a millisecond but requires the sense of a beat that is dimensionless. The drummer's sweet spot is described as being almost mystical, but there is nothing unreal about it. It is a tight and thrillingly exacting feedback loop in which the drummer's attentions are focused on single points of moment-by-moment sound and rhythm. At these times, drummers are utterly removed from themselves and totally immersed in the pleasure of the process.

Computer programmers describe the same sort of entrancement and enhancement of their focus and output. As they write their computer code, to the background sounds of clicking keyboard taps, hackers fall into deep work-flow. This is a time when their minds and the "mind" of the computer are in unison. Linking together a chain of sweet spots, time passes without notice for the programmer, and that feeling is as important as the product they produce.

The sweet spots for families are those times when the components of the entire family, especially the children, are linked together, growing in unison.

Recently, I visited with a couple by the name of Mark and Lynette, who are business partners and friends of mine, and I observed them and their family unit. Their two children were in the Scouts, played on sports teams, made good grades, and dearly loved their parents. Mark and Lynette were happy with each other, worked their business together, shared free time, had ideal physical amenities, and what seemed like a perfect lifestyle.

One afternoon, Mark and I took off for a 10-mile run, and, as we strode over the hills, I said, "It seems so perfect—you

The reason why—a sweet spot in sports.

1991

are living out your values and dreams. Your children are happy and normal; you don't have many problems or worries. There aren't many families that get to be in this sweet spot."

It was just like Mark when he said, "The grass *is* greener on my side of the fence." I was impressed—he was living it, and he knew it at the same time. He wasn't longing for someone else's lifestyle or lawn. Sure, things for him and Lynette aren't always chloroform aseptic green, but these two parents are successfully nurturing and caring for their entire family's chain of sweet spots.

For me, life seems to work like a series of parallel channels, which transmit energy both separately and in tandem. I have six lines or channels—you may have more or less. These six life-paths transmit their energy along the following (non-hierarchical) routes:

FAMILIAL

PROFESSIONAL

FINANCIAL

SOCIAL

SPIRITUAL

ATHLETIC

When it is all working for me, when high levels of positive, healthy energy are traveling down all of my six lines, I am peaking out. It is like the feeling that the athlete, the programmer, and the musician all feel, combined. It is the sweet spot.

In the *Sweet Spot in Time,** one of my favorite authors, John Jerome, describes this point in time as being magic. "It is my thesis—the Sweet Spot Theory—that this is true magic, the only magic there is," writes Jerome.

When you are there—in the sweet spot—it is always in the here-and-now. It is a full immersion into the present moment in time, and the sweetness of that moment is like sugar-coating the magical with the mystical. It's probably part of the answer to the "why" question—why we are alive and why those of us who love what we do—athletics, art, work, relationships— love it so much.

* *Touchstone, Simon and Schuster, Inc., New York, New York, 1980.*

BIBLIOGRAPHY

TRIATHLON BOOKS

Allen, Mark with Bob Babbitt. *Mark Allen's Total Triathlete.* Chicago: Contemporary Books, 1988.

Baker, Erin and John Hellemans. *Triathlon: The Winning Edge.* Auckland: Heinemann Reed, 1988.

Coakley, Jay. *Sport and Society.*

Edwards, Sally. *Triathlon Log.* Sacramento: *FLEET FEET* Press, 1982.

Edwards, Sally. *Triathlon: A Triple Fitness Sport.* Chicago: Contemporary Books, 1983.

Edwards, Sally. *Triathlon Training and Racing.* Chicago: Contemporary Books, 1985.

Edwards, Sally. *Triathlons for Fun.* Santa Monica: Triathlete Magazine, 1992.

Edwards, Sally. *Triathlons for Women.* Santa Monica: Triathlete Magazine, 1992.

Edwards, Sally. *Triathlons for Kids.* Santa Monica: Triathlete Magazine, 1992.

Engelhardt, Martin and Alexandra Kremer. *Triathlon: Technique, Training and Competition.* Great Britain: Springfield Books Limited, 1987.

Horning, Dave and Gerald Couzens. *Triathlon: Lifestyle of Fitness.* New York: Wallaby Books, 1985.

Lachmann, Gunter, and Thomas Steffens. *Triathlon: Die Krone der Ausdauer.* Hilden: Spirodon, 1983. (German)

Montgomery, David L. M.D. *The Triathlon Handbook.* New York: Leisure Press. 1983.

Plant, Mike. *Iron Will: The Heart and Soul of the Triathlon's Ultimate Challenge.* Chicago: Contemporary Books, 1987.

Perry, Paul. *Paul Perry's Complete Book of the Triathlon.* New York: Plume Books, 1983.

Scott, Dave. *Dave Scott's Triathlon Training.* New York: Simon & Schuster, Inc., 1986.

Sisson, Mark with Ray Hosler. *Runner's World Triathlon Training Book.* California: Anderson World Books, 1983.

Town, Glenn P. *Science of Triathlon Training and Competition.* Illinois: Human Kinetics Publishers, Inc., 1985.

Tri-Fed/USA. *1990 Triathlon Competition Guide.* Colorado: Tri-Fed/USA, 1990.

Vaz, Katherine and Barclay Kruse. *The High-Performance Triathlete.* Chicago: Contemporary Books, 1985.

Vaz, Katherine. *Cross-Training: The Complete Book of the Triathlon.* New York: Avon Books, 1984.

RECOMMENDED READING FOR CHILDREN

FICTION (primary)

Alborough, Jez, *Running Bear*

Carlson, Nancy, *Loudmouth George and the Big Race*

Delton, Judy, *Bear and Duck on the Run*

Eagle, Michael, *The Marathon Rabbit*

Isenberg, Barbara, *The Adventures of Albert, the Running Bear*

Kessler, Leonard, *The Big Mile Race*

Moore, John, *Granny Stickleback*

Sachs, Marilyn, *Fleet Footed Florence*

Wiseman, *The Lucky Runner*

FICTION (intermediate)

Adoff, Arnold, *I am the Running Girl* (poetry)

Alcock, Gudrun, *Run, Westy, Run*

Coerr, Eleanor, *Sadako and the Thousand Paper Cranes*

Goff, Lloyd Lozes, *Run, Sandpiper, Run*

Harlan, Elizabeth, *Footfalls* (Jr. High)

Iijima Toshiko, *Run, Peepo*

Knudson, R. R., *Fox Running*

Knudson, R. R., *Speed*

Lee, Robert C., *It's a Mile from here to Glory*

Levy, Elizabeth, *Running Out of Magic with Houdini*

Levy, Elizabeth, *Running Out of Time*

Matthew, Christopher, *Run, Billy, Run* (Jr. High)

McClinton, Leon, *Cross Country Runner*

Morey, Walter, *Run Far, Run Fast*

Osborne, Mary Pope, *Run, Run as Fast as You Can*

Platt, Kin, *Run for Your Life* (Jr. High)

Robinson, Mabel Louise, *Runner of the Mountain Tops*

Savitz, Harriet May, *Run, Don't Walk*

Sullivan, George, *Run, run fast!*

Wersba, Barbara, *Run Softly, Go Fast*

Winthrop, Elizabeth, *Marathon Miranda*

Woolverton, Linda, *Running Before the Wind*

NON-FICTION

Aaseng, Nathan: *Track's Magnificent Milers*

Biographies of World record breaking mile runners, including Glenn Cunningham, Roger Bannister, Herbert Elliott, Jim Ryun, Kip Keino, John Walker, Filbert Bayi, Sebastian Coe, Steve Ovett, and Mary Decker.

Aaseng, Hathan: *World Class Marathoners*

Outlines history of marathons and careers of seven great marathon runners, including emil Zatopek, Abebe Bikila, Frank Shorter, and Bill Rogers.

Asch, Frank: *Running with Rachel*

Rachel discusses running, including how her interest began, proper shoes, diet, exercises, and competition.

Benjamin, Carol Lee: *Running Basics*

Discusses aspects of running, such as conditioning, techniques, equipment, and injuries.

Fogel, Julianna Wesley: *Paul, Marathon Runner*

Highlights the life of a Chinese American runner, his record breaking performance in the New York City Marathon at the age of nine, and his dream to compete in the Olympics.

Higdon, Hal: *The Marathoners*

Includes biographies stressing the achievements of some outstanding marathon runners of modern times and describes the major marathon events around the world.

Jacobs, Linda Mary Decker: *Speed Records and Spaghetti*

Biography of a California schoolgirl who, by the age of fifteen had already broken world speed records in running.

Jacobs, Linda Wilma Rudolph: *Run for Glory*

Biography of the woman who overcame polio as a child to become the first woman to win 3 gold medals in track in a single Olympics.

Lytle, Richard: *Jogging and Running*

Guide to jogging and running and related benefits and cautions.

Olney, Ross R: *The Young Runner*

Introduction to running. How to start, what to wear, how to avoid bad habits and develop good running technique, and become conditioned for competition.

Sullivan, George: *Better Cross Country Running for Boys and Girls*

Introduction to cross country running, including history, equipment, strategy and how to improve one's performance.

RESOURCE LIST

BICYCLE GUIDE

711 Boylston Street
Boston, MA 02116
$14.90/yr. (9 issues)
800/456-6501

BICYCLING

33 E Minor Street
Emmaus, PA 18098
$17.97/yr. (10 issues)
800/441-7761

CYCLING SCIENCE

916/938-4411
P.O. Box 1510
Mount Shasta, CA 96067
$19.97/yr. (4 issues)

RUNNERS WORLD

33 E. Minor Street
Emmaus, PA 18098
$24/yr. (12 issues)
800/441-7761

RUNNING & FITNESS

9310 Old George Town Road
Bethesda, MD 20814
800/776-2732

RUNNING RESEARCH NEWS

P.O. Box 27041
Lansing, MI 48909
517/394-7953

RUNNING TIMES

P.O. Box 16927
North Hollywood, CA 91615
$18.95/yr. (12 times)
213/858-7100

SWIM MAGAZINE

P.O. Box 45497
Los Angeles, CA 90045
$19/yr. (12 times)
213/674-2120

TRIATHLETE

1415 Third Street, Suite 303
Santa Monica, CA 90401
$23.95/yr. (11 issues)
800/441-1666

TRIATHLON TODAY

P.O. Box 1587
Ann Arbor, MI 48106
$19.95/yr. (9 issues)
800/346-5902

VELONEWS

5595 Arapahoe Ave. Suite G
Boulder, CO 80303
$24.95/yr. (18 issues)
800/825-0061

WINNING

744 Roble Road
Suite 190
Allentown, PA 18103-9100
$23.95/yr. (11 issues)
800/441-1666

RESEARCH GUIDES

1990 Triathlon Competitive Guide

TRI-FED/USA
P.O. Box 1010
Colorado Springs, CO 80901
An Annual Information
Booklet

ORGANIZATIONS

Assoc. of Military Triathletes

64 Rose Hill Drive
Bluffton, SC 29910
803/757-5455

Bicycle Helmet Safety Institute

4649 Second Street S.
Arlington, VA 22204
703/521-2080

Bike Centennial

P.O. Box 8308
Missoula, MT 59807
406/721-1776

**League of American Wheelmen
(LAW)**

6706 Whitestone Rd., Suite 309
Baltimore, MD 21207
301/944-3399

**Melpomene Institute for Women's
Health Research**

1010 University Avenue
St. Paul, MN 55104
612/378-0545

**Road Runner Clubs of America
(RRCA)**

629 S. Washington Street
Alexandria, VA 22314
703/836-0558

The Athletic Congress (TAC)

P.O. Box 120
Indianapolis, IN 46206
317/638-9155

Tri-Canada
>
> 1154 W. 24th Street
> N. Vancouver, BC V6V 2J2
> CANADA
> 604/987-0092

Tri-Fed/USA
>
> MEMBERSHIP APPLICATION
> HOTLINE
> 800/874-1872

Tri-Fed/USA
>
> National Office
> 3595 E. Fountain Blvd.
> P.O. Box 1010
> Colorado Springs, CO 80901
> 719/597-9090

Ultra Marathon Cycling Association
>
> 4790 Irvine Blvd. #105-111
> Irvine, CA 92720
> 714/544-1701

US Amateur, Inc.
>
> 275 East Avenue
> Norwalk, CT 06855
> 800/872-1992 or 203/866-1984

US Cycling Federation
>
> 1750 E. Boulder Street
> Colorado Springs, CO 80909
> 719/578-4581

US Master Swimming
>
> 2 Peter Avenue
> Rutland, MA 01543
> 505/886-6631

USOC Drug Hotline
>
> 800/223-0393

US Swimming
>
> 1750 E. Boulder
> Colorado Springs, CO 80909
> 719/578-4578

Women's Sports Foundation
>
> 342 Madison Ave Suite 728
> New York, NY 10173
> 800-227-3988

TRAINING CAMPS

Camp Fleet Feet
>
> 1555 River Park Drive, Suite 102
> Sacramento, CA 95815
> 916/442-3338

Florida Triathlon Camp
>
> 1447 Peachtree Street NE,
> Suite 804
> Atlanta, GA 30309
> 404/875-6987

John Howard School of Champions
>
> 1705 Old Mill Road
> Encinitas, CA 92024
> 619/753-5894

Midwest Triathlon Training Camp
>
> Jackson Y Center
> 127 West Wesley
> Jackson, MI 49201
> 517/782-0537

National Triathlon Training Camp
>
> 1015 Gayley Ave., Suite 217
> Los Angeles, CA 90024
> 213/478-8304

Triathletics Triathlon and Biathlon Training Camp
>
> Prestige Sports
> P.O. Box 937
> Greenbrook, NJ 08812
> 800/397-1727

Tri-Texas Triathlon Training Camp
>
> c/o THCT, 11855 1H10 West,
> Suite 503
> San Antonio, TX 78230

Vail Cross-Training Camp
    Jim Davis
    P.O. Box 3364
    Vail, CO 81658
    303/476-5968

NATIONAL RACE SERIES

**DANSKIN WOMEN'S TRIATHLON
SERIES**
    212/930-9115

BLTS (BudLight Triathlon Series)
    5966 La Place Ct #100
    Carlsbad, CA 92008
    619/438-8080

**IRONMAN (Hawaii) World Series Race
Office**
    75-170 Hualalai Rd. #D214
    Kailua-Kona, HI 96740
    808/329-0063

IRONMAN (Hawaii)
    Race Office
    75-170 Hualalai Rd. #D214
    Kailua-Kona, HI 96740
    808/329-0063 FAX: 808/326-2131

IRONMAN Mainland Office
    World Triathlon Corporation
    1570 US Hwy 19N
    Tarpon Springs, FL 34689
    813/942-4767

RAINBO IRONKIDS Race Series
    Track Sports
    P.O. Box 69095
    St. Louis, MO 63169
    314/241-8100

SALLY EDWARDS

Founder & President
FLEET FEET, Incorporated, a national franchise corporation with 40 retail sports stores.

Author
Triathlons for Women (1992)
Triathlons for Fun (1992)
Triathlons for Kids (1992)
The Triathlon Training and Racing Book (1985)

The Equilibrium Plan (1987)
Triathlon: A Triple Fitness Sport (1982)
The Woman Runner's Training Diary (1983)

Syndicated Columnist
Sally Edwards' Women's Sports Column.

Professional Athlete
Current Master's Ironman World Record Holder and thirteen-time Ironman Triathlon finisher.
Olympic Marathon trials Qualifier—1984.
Winner of the 1980 Western States 100-mile run and three-time finisher.
Three-time winner of the Levi Ride and Tie.
Winner of the American River 50 Miler (1980 and 1983).

Journalist
Over 100 magazine articles published.

Television Personality
KXTV-CBS television special sports commentator.
PM Magazine national special feature "Sally Edwards, The Woman Who Runs 100 Miles."

Spokesperson
Danskin Women's Triathlon Series Spokesperson (1990–91, 1991–92)
NIKE, Inc. sponsored athlete
General Foods national media tour 1984 and 1985

Academic Degrees
National University in Business (M.B.A., 1986) University of California, Berkeley, Exercise Physiology (M.A., 1970)

Memberships
Trustee, Women's Sports Foundation
Woman's Forum

Personal
After completing graduate school in Berkeley, Sally served with the American Red Cross in Vietnam. Returning home in 1972, she taught for three years before taking her entrepreneurial spirit forward and co-founding *FLEET FEET SPORTS.* Today, at the age of 44, she resides in Sacramento, California, living the fitness lifestyle as an athlete, businesswoman, author, journalist, and professional speaker.

Rainbo Bread
Ironkids National
Championships

Dallas, Texas
September 29–30, 1991
(7–10) 100-meter swim, 5k bike, 1k run
(11–14) 200-meter swim, 10k bike, 2k run

IRONKIDS—JUNIOR GIRLS
AGE GROUP RESULTS

GIRLS TOP FIVE JUNIORS

1	Jennifer Capelli	0:18:23
2	Carrie Tindol	0:18:25
3	Monique Melara	0:19:18
4	Ann Robbins	0:19:40
5	Shannon Rhodes	0:19:41

GIRLS AGE GROUP: 7

1	Emily Finnessy	0:25:07
2	Megan von Fange	0:28:00
3	Shawna Bourdon	0:28:39
4	Meredith Hominick	0:31:03

GIRLS AGE GROUP: 8

1	Bethany Brovey	0:21:12
2	Michelle Baxter	0:21:13
3	Lauren Wencel	0:21:48
4	Jamie Sisler	0:21:50
5	Sarah Bickerstaff	0:23:52

GIRLS AGE GROUP: 9

1	Ann Robbins	0:19:40
2	Melanie Gast	0:19:45
3	Kim Jones	0:20:42
4	Meghan Melton	0:21:50
5	Karen Baumeister	0:22:40

GIRLS AGE GROUP: 10

1	Jennifer Capelli	0:18:23
2	Carrie Tindol	0:18:25
3	Monique Melara	0:19:18
4	Shannon Rhodes	0:19:41
5	Erin Giesa	0:19:49

IRONKIDS SENIOR GIRLS
AGE GROUP RESULTS

GIRLS TOP FIVE SENIORS

1	Katy Radkewich	0:33:41
2	Jennifer Bossert	0:34:22
3	Nichole Hartman	0:34:31
4	Sara Turtle	0:35:58
5	Maureen Kennedy	0:36:06

GIRLS AGE GROUP: 11

1	Sara Brinkley	0:36:39
2	Jocelyn Keller	0:37:31
3	Terri Schwager	0:39:39
4	Katie Willengerg	0:40:38
5	Mikki Reading	0:42:32

GIRLS AGE GROUP: 12

1	Katy Radkewich	0:33:41
2	Kristina Kehoe	0:37:30
3	Katie Reichardt	0:37:54
4	Lisa Cummins	0:38:48
5	Regina Wilhelm	0:38:54

GIRLS AGE GROUP: 13

1	Jennifer Bossert	0:34:22
2	Natalie Nelson	0:36:50
3	Jamie Dvorak	0:36:56
4	Jamie Walker	0:37:00
5	Jessica Hoke	0:37:05

GIRLS AGE GROUP: 14

1	Nichole Hartman	0:34:31
2	Sara Turtle	0:35:58
3	Maureen Kennedy	0:36:06
4	Megan Farrell	0:36:07
5	Stacy Poole	0:36:20

IRONKIDS JUNIOR BOYS AGE GROUP RESULTS

BOYS TOP FIVE JUNIORS
1	Matthew Rother	0:17:51
2	Andy Gardner	0:18:02
3	Brian Custon	0:18:10
4	Heath Duke	0:18:36
5	Sean McCarty	0:18:50

BOYS AGE GROUP: 7
1	Christopher Eddy	0:21:15
2	Allen Duvall	0:22:05
3	Matthew Kukla	0:22:15
4	Matthew Lowry	0:22:24
5	Ryan Sharp	0:24:08

BOYS AGE GROUP: 8
1	David Douglas	0:19:44
2	Neal Papevies	0:19:45
3	Jordan Malinovsky	0:19:59
4	Jake Muhleisen	0:20:12
5	Kohle Heimlich	0:21:48

BOYS AGE GROUP: 9
1	Sean McCarty	0:18:50
2	Brent Hitchcock	0:19:12
3	Ben Mooney	0:19:29
4	Kevin Heath	0:19:29
5	James Lovewell	0:19:36

BOYS AGE GROUP: 10
1	Matthew Rother	0:17:51
2	Andy Gardner	0:18:02
3	Brian Cutson	0:18:10
4	Heath Duke	0:18:36
5	Brett Schumann	0:19:00

IRONKIDS SENIOR BOYS AGE GROUP RESULTS

BOYS TOP FIVE SENIORS
1	Neal Herman	0:31:18
2	Joshua Fuller	0:31:39
3	Ryan Slater	0:31:46
4	Joey Capelli	0:31:51
5	Ryan Posener	0:32:41

BOYS AGE GROUP: 11
1	Bryan Rother	0:34:48
2	Michael Eddy	0:35:18
3	Matt Miller	0:36:25
4	Darrell Quandt	0:36:33
5	Chris Daniels	0:36:38

BOYS AGE GROUP: 12
1	Bryan Hayes	0:33:02
2	Mark Frieser	0:33:09
3	Neil Phippen	0:35:53
4	Andy Mullenix	0:36:10
5	Dustin Lee	0:36:16

BOYS AGE GROUP: 13
1	Nat Faulkner	0:33:52
2	August Pfluger	0:34:50
3	Sean Murray	0:35:26
4	Phillip Briggs	0:35:32
5	Jace Graham	0:36:17

BOYS AGE GROUP: 14
1	Neal Herman	0:31:18
2	Joshua Fuller	0:31:39
3	Ryan Slater	0:31:46
4	Joey Capelli	0:31:51
5	Ryan Posener	0:32:41